The Practical Mystic

OTHER BOOKS BY NEROLI DUFFY

A Journey Through Cancer:
A Woman Doctor's Personal Experience
with Breast Cancer

Wanting to Be Born:
The Cry of the Soul

Wanting to Live:
Overcoming the Seduction of Suicide

BOOKS BY ANNICE BOOTH

The Path to Your Ascension:
Rediscovering Life's Ultimate Purpose

Secrets of Prosperity:
Abundance in the 21st Century

Memories of Mark:
My Life with Mark Prophet

The Practical Mystic

Life-Lessons from
Conversations with Mrs. Booth

Neroli Duffy

Darjeeling Press
Emigrant, Montana

THE PRACTICAL MYSTIC:
Life-Lessons from Conversations with Mrs. Booth
by Neroli Duffy
Copyright © 2009 by Neroli Duffy
All rights reserved

For information, please contact:
Darjeeling Press
PO Box 154, Emigrant, MT 59027, USA
www.darjeelingpress.com

ISBN: 978-0-9824997-0-2

Cover photo:
Annice Booth in 2003 signing a newly-released book.

For additional photographs of Annice and her life,
and for a reading group guide,
please see our web site.

I dedicate this book to Annice Booth and her teachers—Morya, Serapis Bey, Mark and Mother. It is my hope that by the grace of God, they might be pleased with this offering.

ACKNOWLEDGMENTS

Many thanks to:

Annice, mentor and friend,
for sharing your stories with me, having
the courage to allow me to tell them, and for
reading through and editing this manuscript
numerous times.

Linda Worobec and Susan Kulp for their
valuable insights, critique and comments
along the way.

Joyce Canady for selflessly proofing and
reviewing the final manuscript.

Peter, dear co-worker and husband,
for all your work in making this book
the best it could be.

TABLE OF CONTENTS

Contents

Contents

Introduction

I came to know Annice Booth in the early 1990s, when I worked for her for several years. In time we became friends, rather than just employer and employee. Over the years our assignments changed, and we saw less of one another. Then one day in early 1999 I called her and asked if she would like to go to lunch in nearby Yellowstone Park. She said in her characteristic way, "I'm available!"

I bundled up against the cold and drove down to pick her up so we could go on our little adventure. On this occasion, we went to the grand old hotel at Mammoth Hot Springs, one of her favorite spots for lunch. The view was beautiful and the mountain air invigorating. Annice always felt better in the higher altitude of the Park—it was as if she could really breathe there. She also loved to see the bison, deer and elk.

Thus began a series of weekly outings, going to Mammoth or Chico Hot Springs or Pine Creek, or sometimes further afield to Livingston, Bozeman and beyond. Our outings were usually an hour or two, often over lunch. In winter we usually went to Gardiner, the small town at the north entrance of Yellowstone Park. Gardiner can be pretty quiet in winter when the tourists are gone and most of the restaurants are closed.

But the Town Cafe was always open, with its laminated table-tops, vinyl seats, colorful locals, moose and elk trophies on the walls and good home cooking.

Annice loved food and her friends enjoyed taking her out to eat. She was good company, always interesting and informative. Sprinkled here and there were stories of her life, and in particular, her experiences with Mark and Elizabeth Prophet, spiritual teachers and pioneers in the New Age movement in America. Annice met Mark and Elizabeth in 1966, only a few years after the founding of their organization, The Summit Lighthouse. She joined their staff in 1969.

Mark and Elizabeth were messengers for the ascended masters, who are the saints and sages of East and West, brothers and sisters of light who have graduated from earth's schoolroom throughout the ages and returned to God in the ritual of the ascension. The messengers delivered the teachings of the masters to the world in the form of lectures in their own words and dictations from the masters themselves.

The early days of the organization were a remarkable time —a small circle of students living in the household of their teachers, almost in the tradition of the spiritual communities of the East. Was it also something like this for the disciples and the holy women who were with Jesus in the Holy Land? Or for the brothers and sisters of Francis and Clare when they had just a small band at Assisi?

Annice had many fascinating stories to tell of her interactions with the messengers and the masters. They provided insights into a life that few are fortunate enough to experience. They shed light on the spiritual path and what it means to be a modern-day mystic.

After Mark Prophet ascended in 1973, Elizabeth carried

on his work and grew the organization to become a worldwide movement with outposts on every continent. Annice was a part of that growth and saw and learned much. She became an author and editor, a minister in Church Universal and Triumphant, and the director of two teaching centers. Eventually she was placed in charge of ministering to the members of the organization around the world.

Through all of this, Annice was a dedicated student of the masters' teachings. She kept her own files and had a phenomenal memory for where a particular gem from the masters had been published. But more than this, she was a student of the masters themselves, and also the messengers who were their representatives to the world.

As our outings continued, the stories kept coming. Eventually I started to write them down. They were so unique and precious and I did not want them to be lost. I took notes when I could to record all the details, hurrying to keep up with the flow of her thoughts. Often she would pause, as if dictating, to allow me to catch up. I took to carrying a notebook with me whenever I met her, because I never knew when a story would emerge.

A few years later I told Annice that her stories should be published so that others could also learn from them. She said, "I have already written down all that I dare to write in my three books." She was referring to *Memories of Mark, Secrets of Prosperity* and *The Path to Your Ascension*. She said she could not print these stories or even tell them to others, since they involved private details of her life with the messengers. Even more than this, some of the experiences were in the Zen nature of the Eastern tradition of the Guru-chela relationship. Annice thought they would not be understood or appreciated by those who had not experienced this first-hand.

I told her I felt that these stories could be understood if they were explained and put in context. The lessons were so valuable for anyone who was serious about a spiritual path. If they were not written down, I feared that they would be lost, and with them, some wonderful practical examples of the reality of the Guru-chela relationship with the ascended masters.

I told Annice many times, "You may not be able to tell your stories, but I know that I could." Finally she relented, saying, "Publish them when I am gone. Write them down and after I am gone decide how much you dare put into a book." I quickly agreed before she changed her mind, and thus this book began. Later, when she saw the manuscript, she urged me to publish it while she was still with us.

The stories you will find here illustrate what Annice understood of the spiritual path and what motivated her to persist on that path all these years. They are mystical, and yet the lessons they illustrate have very practical application. Most especially they offer examples of a living chelaship under two remarkable spiritual teachers. To me, these stories are now more important than ever, when Mark is no longer with us in the physical and Elizabeth has retired from outer service for health reasons.

I asked myself one day why I took so long to begin to write down the stories that Annice told me. I treasured them and thought to myself that "someone" should write them down some day. Annice was always focused on her current projects (a lesson in chelaship in itself), and she had a kind of timeless quality that made it hard to imagine a time when she would not be here with us. But by 2002 Annice was eighty-two, and no one had yet taken that torch. I finally decided that maybe it should be me.

Perhaps I was prompted by someone upstairs who wanted it done. I would not be surprised if it was Lanello (the name by which we know Mark Prophet now that he is an ascended master). She knew him for six years before he ascended and he seems to take a special interest in her to this day, making sure that her needs are met. Many of Annice's friends remember getting an inner prompting to call her and then finding that she needed something done. It was not uncommon for me to call and ask if she wanted to go to lunch, only to hear her say, "Good, I told Lanello that I needed to get out."

I am glad that I wrote the stories down when I did, for in February 2007 Annice suffered a stroke. Although she remained the same person she had always been, the stroke severely limited her ability to speak and write. For someone whose whole life had been speaking and writing, it was humbling to have to start all over again, to learn to speak in words that made sense and to learn to write again, beginning with signing her name.

Yet Annice could still make herself understood. She even retained her sense of humor under what would have been very frustrating circumstances for most people. She would know exactly what she wanted to say, but try as she might the words often came out all jumbled. Her friends admired her good humor, fortitude and sheer determination. We often had to play twenty questions to figure out exactly what she meant. She commented that even if she and I had wanted to write down her stories, she was now simply no longer able to do so.

I am passing on these stories as she told them to me and as I have reconstructed them from my notes. I have also added commentary giving my understanding of the lessons in chelaship that they convey. They are in loosely chronological order, but the sequence isn't all that important. They came forth originally as the Holy Spirit prompted her to reveal them, each one an important little lesson in the Guru-chela relationship, and they do stand alone as individual vignettes of the path.

Annice has been a chela of the masters and the messengers for more than forty years. She has seen times when some seemed to forget what chelaship was all about and others appeared to be failing tests and falling by the wayside. Those who follow in her footsteps may not have the blessing of the one-on-one relationship with the messengers that she was fortunate to experience on the outer, but this relationship is still possible on the inner. Those who want to take up this path have a wealth of knowledge in the teachings of the messengers and the masters. They also have the example of Annice and of many others who have made it on the path. All of these can provide guideposts to a very rich relationship with the Guru on inner levels.

I knew early in the process of compiling this book that it would not be a complete account of Annice's life. That would take a book in itself. Although I have included biographical details and photographs, the main focus is the tale of a unique and often misunderstood relationship—that between master and disciple, between student and teacher.

It is my hope that these few vignettes from my conversations with Mrs. Booth will provide encouragement and inspiration for others to pursue the path of chelaship under the ascended masters, with all of its challenges and joys.

Neroli Duffy

CHAPTER 1

The Path of Chelaship

In the Eastern tradition, a student who wishes to pursue the spiritual path seeks out a master, a Guru, who can teach the sacred mysteries and impart to the chela the initiations leading to enlightenment. The Ascended Master El Morya defines chelaship in his classic book on this subject, *The Chela and the Path*:

> In the Eastern tradition of chelaship, recognized for thousands of years as the way of self-mastery and enlightenment, one desiring to have the mysteries of universal law imparted to him applies to the Teacher, known as the Guru, considered to be a Master (through the ages the real gurus have included both ascended and unascended Masters) to serve that Teacher until he is found worthy to receive the keys to his own inner reality....
>
> In return for illumined obedience and self-sacrificing love, the chela receives increments of the Master's attainment—of the Master's own realization of his

Real Self. Through the acceptance of the word of the Master as inviolate, the chela has imparted to him the Christ consciousness of his Master, which in turn is the means whereby the base elements of the chela's subconscious and the momentums of his untransmuted karma are melted by the fervent heat of the sacred fire which comprises the Master's consciousness.

Thus, by freely and willingly setting aside the momentums of his human consciousness, the chela discovers that these are soon replaced by his Teacher's mastery, which, when he makes it his own, serves as the magnet to magnetize his own higher consciousness and attainment.

Chelaship has been described as a unique inner relationship between the master and the student. The goal for the chela is the reunion with the Higher Self in the ritual known as the ascension. It is a free-will relationship, somewhat like a marriage contract, where the two are bonded and the master works to mold the student in the image and likeness of his or her Christ Self. The means are any mode or method that the master can use to take the chela where he or she needs to go to bypass the human condition and to embrace the divine.

The relationship between Guru and chela, or Master and disciple in the terminology of the West, has always been central to the spiritual path. In the East, people tend to think of the Guru as necessarily being in the physical plane, and those who were serious about the spiritual path would earnestly seek out the one who could open the door for them.

In the West the Guru-chela relationship is not seen so often in the physical, yet there are some notable examples, perhaps most famously in the case of Jesus and his disciples. In the fragments of this relationship found in the Bible, Jesus appears very much in the mode of the Guru. He transmits to the disciples the keys to higher consciousness; he sets the rules for their discipleship; he rebukes them when necessary.

And of course, their relationship with him does not end when he leaves the scene in Palestine. He continues to teach them, to guide them, to initiate them.

Many Christians today understand Jesus to be their Lord and Saviour. They might not be comfortable with thinking of him as Guru, but he is their Lord, their Master. They might not think of themselves as chelas, but they are striving to be, or are, disciples, and they have a living relationship with the Master Jesus, now ascended. I have met people who have this very real tie with Jesus. As they walk the spiritual path, they are aware of his guidance and direction. This is a mystical and yet very real relationship that we can all aspire to have with Jesus, or with another of the ascended masters.

The training on the path of chelaship, whether inner or outer, is individual for each student, yet certain elements are always the same. It is very much on-the-job training. The master will use the lessons that circumstances and one's karma present at any moment on the road of life. The training may be rigorous as the master seeks to wrestle with the human creation of the student. The student is expected to observe himself and to change his behavior when it is not acceptable or pleasing to the master. It is a practical path, designed to lead the student to the goal of the ascension.

Above all, the Guru-chela relationship is a relationship of profound and intense love. The love of the Guru and the chela surpasses any relationship of love that is known on this planet —even that of husband and wife. For in truth, the highest form of relationship between husband and wife is also a guru-chela relationship where each is subject to the Christ Self of the other.

Taking on a chela is not done lightly by a master. For in so doing, the master literally takes the karma of the chela and bears a portion of it himself. In turn the chela pledges to serve the master and his mission in the world, part of which is often to reach those who are also tied to the master at inner levels but do not yet know it on the outer.

This book seeks to describe that which is in some ways indescribable. It tries to shine a light on aspects of the Guru-chela relationship through the eyes of one who went through it and witnessed it first hand—not a perfect chela (for there is no such thing) but one who has endured on the path to the end.

The ascended masters have said that those who were trained by the messengers should also pass on their training to others. Annice lamented that in later years this form of training was often not welcomed or accepted. One reason for this may be a lack of understanding of the masters and their methods, which are often counterintuitive to the human mind because they are designed to outsmart that mind as well as the not-self.

Perhaps this book will in some way help to fulfill this request from the masters. Those of us who knew Annice have learned much from the stories she told of her life with the messengers and the gems of truth that they contain. These stories give a glimpse into the lives of the messengers, two special souls who spanned the octaves of heaven and earth. And most importantly, they give a unique insight into the relationship between the Guru and the chela and the time-honored methods by which the masters have trained their students through the ages. For the messengers do hold the office of Guru, even while they are the representatives of the ascended masters, who are the true Gurus of this age.

Annice serves on the fourth ray, the ray of purity and discipline—qualities that were very evident in her life. Her Guru is Serapis Bey, the chohan of the fourth ray. According to Cosmic Law, you can only have one Guru at a time. But the Guru may send a chela to another ascended master for a time.

For example, many of the masters send those who come to them as would-be chelas to El Morya, since he has a great skill in the training of new students. Thus in some of the episodes that Annice recounts, El Morya appears as the Guru. He is the founder of The Summit Lighthouse and the Guru of the messengers, very much involved in the day-to-day activities of the organization.

The masters also deliver their initiations and training through the messengers as their representatives in the physical plane. So Annice also received her training in chelaship from Mark Prophet and from Elizabeth, who we know as Mother.

There is a great bond between Mark, Mother and Annice, one that endures beyond time and space. Annice promised Mark that she would remain faithful to Mother and would remain with her while she was in embodiment. Some of us suspect that this is one of the reasons Annice has remained in embodiment for so many years and why she is still with us.

The ascended masters and the messengers are very present spiritually in this time and the Guru-chela relationship is as real and vital today as it ever was. For those who wish to pursue this relationship, Annice's stories provide some unique lessons.

Let's begin with a brief look at her life.

MORYA

MARK

MOTHER

MRS. BOOTH

CHAPTER 2

Snapshots from the Life of a Chela

Annice Elma Moore was born on May 28, 1920. Annice never liked the name Elma, but Mark said that you cannot get closer to El Morya than El Ma Moore. He explained that *El Ma* means "mother of God," and Moore was the name of one of Morya's embodiments.

Annice describes her childhood as a happy one. She had two sisters—one of whom died at an early age due to a genetic disposition to heart disease. Annice inherited the same condition but broke out of that mold in a spectacular way.

She attended the University of California in Berkeley and majored in Latin and French. She wanted to be a teacher, but did not finish her degree. She was also a serious Bible student and could quote scripture—book, chapter and verse.

Annice married Lester Booth on May 30, 1940, two days after her twentieth birthday. Her father lost his job three weeks before the wedding and he had no savings. He was a meat buyer for the Andrew Williams chain of stores. He called in an efficiency expert, who promptly decided that they could

Annice at nine months. When Mother saw this picture of Annice she said, "This is a serious soul!" Annice was known for being serious and disciplined. Each one of us was born to serve on one of the seven rainbow rays of God. Annice served on the white ray of God's purity, discipline and love. That discipline shows through in this picture.

Annice in 1938, an eighteen-year-old sophomore. This was her engagement picture.

do without Annice's father. Annice said, "He efficienced himself out of a job!"

The big wedding she had planned in a large church in Hayward, California, was scaled back to a more intimate occasion at home. Annice, as always, was adaptable. They moved the organ to the living room and the bride walked down the aisle from the kitchen. The number of guests was reduced to about thirty.

Lester owned a photography studio in Hayward. After they married Annice went to work at the studio. At this point she became "Mrs. Booth." It was a name that would stick for a lifetime.

Annice's son, Lawrence William Booth (Little Larry), arrived on April 28, 1943. Larry was Annice's only child and she considers that she was lucky to have him. Her doctors had told her earlier that because of her health problems, including thyroid disease and myasthenia gravis, she could never have children. But Annice didn't give up. She so much wanted to have a child.

Mother once told Annice that she had searched the karmic records and there was no indication that Annice and Larry had any connection, good or bad. There was no karma between them at all. This is very unusual, since most families come together with ties from past lives. Often they are working out their past negative karma together; sometimes positive momentums from the past are a foundation for service together in this one. But Annice and Larry had never been together in any past lives and there was no earthly reason why she should be his mother. Annice says that she basically pestered God until he gave her this little boy. The Karmic Board, the spiritual overseers who oversee these things, finally said, "All

Annice on her wedding day. Annice said of this photograph "What a picture of innocence if ever you saw it." Her purity certainly shines through. This photograph is taken in her family home, where the wedding took place.

Annice took this photograph of her son, "Little Larry," while her husband, Lester, was away in Guam during World War II. Lester was the photographer in the family and she was proud that she could be behind the camera for once. She had never taken a photograph before, let alone printed one, but she set the whole thing up herself and developed the film in the closet. She was very pleased with herself. Even Lester admitted that Annice "did a good job."

Annice and her son, Larry. It was not in Annice's divine plan to have children in this life, but like the woman in Jesus' parable of the unjust judge, Annice prayed so earnestly to have a child that the Karmic Board finally granted her request.

During World War II Annice went to San Diego to say good-bye to Lester when he was sent to Guam.

right. Let's give her a child."

In addition to raising their son, Annice and Lester ran the photography studio from 1958 to 1969. Annice was successful in business. She never lacked for abundance. In later life, she would comment how the money seemed to grow in her bank account. She put it to good use. Never extravagant, she always had everything she needed, a self-described simple soul who could be happy almost anywhere. When in later years she wrote her book *Secrets of Prosperity,* she outlined the keys to her success in life and told some of the lessons she had learned from her years in business. It was a very practical application of the thirteen steps to prosperity taught by Mark Prophet.

Annice has a somewhat Buddhic nature hidden within a seemingly ordinary exterior. She is flexible and moves with the Holy Spirit. If something changes, she just says, "That's the way it goes," and moves on. She would need that flexibility all too soon. Her life changed dramatically when she found the Teachings of the Ascended Masters and the messengers Mark L. Prophet and Elizabeth Clare Prophet.

In October 1966 her sister showed her a brochure from The Summit Lighthouse that said, "Jesus is inviting you to have lunch with him in the garden." She felt the call of the master and attended the Harvest Class in Colorado Springs. From the moment she met Mark and Elizabeth, she felt she was home, and she became an active member of the organization. She regularly attended conferences and seminars, and she accompanied the messengers on their European Tour in August and September of 1968.

Mark Prophet invited Annice to join the staff of The Summit Lighthouse in 1969. She wanted to accept Mark's offer but initially declined because she was so busy with the photography studio. But eventually, at the age of forty-nine, she closed her business and joined staff. Lester joined staff a while later.

Annice served in many different capacities in her years on the messengers' staff. The month that she joined, the organization acquired a property in Santa Barbara that would be known as the Motherhouse of the Keepers of the Flame Fraternity. Annice's first job was to supervise the staff who tackled the huge task of painting and remodeling to make the property a beautiful home for the masters. The Motherhouse formally opened Easter 1970, and Annice was placed in charge of this new outpost of the organization in California. She purchased the food, cooked meals, cleaned, supervised staff, conducted services and did whatever else needed to be done.

This willingness to serve in any capacity and meet the need of the hour is one of Annice's characteristics, and she wore many different hats in the early years. She answered the phones, handled correspondence, mailed the *Pearls of Wisdom,* taught at Ascended Master University and was even the principal of Montessori International at one time. For a while she commuted between Santa Barbara and Colorado Springs, continuing to run the Motherhouse while helping Mark and Mother complete their landmark publication *Climb the Highest Mountain.*

She traveled extensively with Mark and Elizabeth, accompanying the messengers and their staff on several tours around the world, including the India Pilgrimage in April 1970 (right after the opening of the Motherhouse), the Holy Land Tour in September and October 1972, and Mission South America in December 1973.

Mother frequently told Annice that she was family, even

Annice in 1947, age twenty-seven. In this photograph I see a sweet and simple quality and a quiet spirituality.

Annice with Mom, Pop, Grandma and Uncle Charlie, who planned to live to be a hundred years old. He was ninety-seven in this picture. When he got to ninety-eight he said, "It just isn't worth it," and died soon after.

The 1967 Christmas card from Les Booth Photography Studios. Lester, Annice and Larry and the family business

Annice Booth, the successful business-woman. This photograph was taken for an appearance as a guest speaker at a conference of the Professional Photographers of America.

though Annice was very clear about who was Guru. She shared many intimate moments with the messengers, even helping Mother raise her youngest child.

In February 1973, Mark Prophet made his transition, going on to become the Ascended Master Lanello. Mark's departure was a great loss to Mother and the staff. They no longer had his personal presence with them. Annice was no exception to this sense of loss, and she felt Mark's absence keenly. Staff life was an intimate, almost family experience for them all. But encouraged by Mother's example, the staff rallied to carry on the mission that beloved Mark had begun, to bring the Teachings of the Ascended Masters to the world.

Annice was ordained as minister in The Summit Lighthouse on July 4, 1974, at a conference held in Spokane, Washington. Many have benefited from her practical spiritual counsel since that time. She was someone you could go to for a no-nonsense perspective.

Under the direction of the messenger, she ministered to a worldwide movement from 1978 to 1982 as the head of the Office of the National Coordinator, later renamed the Office of Ministry. By this time she was divorced from Lester, and the work took her around the world, lecturing, counseling, directing and visiting the study groups and teaching centers on every continent. She considers that it was a time of balancing world karma.

Annice was a faculty member of Summit University for more than twenty years. She taught a course on the laws of the abundant life on Wednesdays, the day of the fifth ray, wearing a long green robe, the color of abundance and healing. She read her lectures from handwritten note cards with carefully chosen quotes, teachings and affirmations from the messengers and the masters. Her course on the ascension followed the same format and was popular with generations of students.

Her ascension class, "The Path to the Ascension," was always on Friday, the day of the amplification of the fourth ray, the ray of the ascension flame. She arrived at 8:30 A.M. sharp wearing her white robe. Annice started promptly and ended exactly on time. Tardy students soon became acquainted with a practical demonstration of the discipline and attention to detail of the fourth ray. She would say, "Young man, do you have a watch? They sell them at the bookstore!" Few students were late twice.

In April 1980 Annice traveled with Mother and other staff members to India to establish the Ashram of the World Mother in New Delhi. In May she traveled as school principal with Mother and Montessori International students to Washington D.C., England, Scotland and Ireland.

Annice was director of the two teaching centers in the Twin Cities of Minneapolis and Saint Paul from 1982 until 1989. One staff member who served there describes her as a "very dear friend who stands up for your soul to support you." Annice was indeed a friend of your soul—and not your human creation, with which she could be stern. She touched many lives throughout her long years of service.

It was in Minneapolis that Annice was suddenly forced to step back for a while from her busy schedule of service. In October 1988 she suffered a major heart attack. Then, when she was in the hospital recovering, she had a cardiac arrest. For twelve minutes the hospital staff worked to revive her while the ascended master Lanello and his twin flame, Mother, were on inner levels discussing Annice's fate.

Lanello wanted her in heaven; Mother wanted her to stay

Annice in 1970,
her passport
photo for
the India
Pilgrimage

Annice at her desk
at the Pasadena
campus, which was
the headquarters
of the organiza-
tion from 1976 to
1978. We do not
know the date,
but we know it
was a Tuesday
because her dress
is blue, the color
of the ray for
that day.

The India Pilgrimage, April 1970. Annice is preparing to give *prasad*, holy offering, at a shrine.

Riding a camel in Egypt, on the Holy Land Tour, September 1972

on earth. In describing this event later, Mother said there are so many saints in heaven, she couldn't understand why God would need another one there when there is so much that needs to be done down here.

Eventually Mother won. Annice was resuscitated and returned to the land of the living. The surgeons opened her chest to perform several bypass grafts. When she was recovering from the surgery, they were amazed to find that she had *no* post-operative pain.

After Annice came back, people asked her what she remembered of her time on the "other side." She said that she remembered looking at the clock on the wall of her room. The next thing she remembered was looking at the clock again and it was twelve minutes later. Her room was full of people and her chest hurt. (They had been pounding on it doing CPR to revive her.) She didn't remember any of what had happened during her near-death experience—no tunnel of light, no meeting with masters and beings of light. She said, "I don't think there is any hope for me. I remember nothing."

We were told at the time that part of the reason for Annice's heart attack was the weight of condemnation upon her. Various people were angry at her for the disciplinarian approach she used in running the teaching center in the Twin Cities. But we also understood that Annice had been granted a dispensation to extend her life. All she knew was that God had sent her back to earth, and therefore she must have more work to do.

On March 15, 1989, at Mother's invitation Annice stepped down as director of the Minneapolis Teaching Center and came to serve at the Royal Teton Ranch in southwest Montana, the international headquarters of The Summit Lighthouse and

Annice home from the hospital in November 1988 following her heart attack and twelve minutes on the "other side." She is recovering in her "mansion by the lake," the teaching center on Lake Harriet in Minneapolis known as Minnehaha House.

In 1989, after recovering from her heart attack. Note the cake with strawberries in front of her (Annice's favorite dessert) and the map of the world behind her. She was about to begin a new phase of her world service.

Church Universal and Triumphant. This spiritual community, known as the Inner Retreat, became her home. She began working once again on Mother's writing and publishing team.

By October 1990 Annice was working as hard as ever. She became the director of the Office of Ministry and soon took on added responsibilities for outreach coordination, Summit University, and rapidly expanding translations and fundraising teams. In a real sense Annice ministered to the world, and the messenger considered that she was "mother to the teaching centers and study groups." She was a prolific letter writer, and at one time or another she visited almost every major center.

She was an excellent administrator and delegator. She did not do anything herself if she could delegate it to someone else, and this is one secret of her success. It took three people to replace her when she retired. By her constancy and faithful support of the mission of the messengers, year in and year out, Annice demonstrated the qualities of perseverance and endurance. Saint Germain once told us that the one quality he wanted from his chelas was endurance.[1] Mother told us that it takes profound love to endure on the path, and Annice certainly endured.

In a dictation on May 28, 1993, the Maha Chohan, the ascended master who is the representative of the Holy Spirit, said to Annice, "The Darjeeling Council salutes our co-worker Rev. Annice Booth and does wish her a happy birthday." This was a very rare honor, since the ascended masters seldom referred to any student by name in a dictation. This salutation shows the esteem with which the Brotherhood held Annice. Mother often told Annice that she was closer to heaven than to earth.

For five years Annice bore the weight of the world on her

On the occasion of Annice's seventy-third birthday, the messenger gave her a framed picture of the Maha Chohan, perhaps a remembrance of the dictation by the Maha Chohan where he extended birthday greetings to her.

Annice at her seventy-seventh birthday party, with some of her "ladies in waiting."

shoulders as she was responsible for overseeing so many aspects of the worldwide organization. But in time, this took its toll on her health. In 1995 she was seventy-five and had had double pneumonia and congestive cardiac failure. Morya told her through Mother that she could not sign one more letter or document or piece of paper, that he did not want that burden on her heart. He told her that she should retire from all responsibilities in the departments where she worked. (However, she continued to serve as a member of the Board of Directors of Church Universal and Triumphant, an office she had held from January 28, 1991, until April 30, 1998.)

With her new freedom, Annice's health soon recovered. But then she got bored! Annice is happiest when she is working, doing something positive for the world and the masters. Years earlier she had dedicated the remainder of her life, "as long as God wants me to remain in embodiment," to spreading the Teachings of the Ascended Masters to the lightbearers of the world. She wasn't about to let retirement stand in the way of her mission, so she settled down to write her first book, *The Path to Your Ascension.*

Annice relates that at one point it seemed that the book was just not coming together. She made the calls to go to El Morya's retreat at Darjeeling that night. The next morning she woke with a first sentence for the book running through her mind. She quickly got up and wrote it down before she forgot, and pretty soon she had written out the whole first chapter, sitting there in her nightgown.

She was inspired to re-write the chapters as if they were lessons in the etheric retreat of Serapis Bey, the Ascension Temple at Luxor. The story just flowed and she was on her way. After the publication of this book, the Ascended Master

Djwal Kul commented on it: "Now you have the book that was written by your teacher Annice Booth. And so you have something that is magnanimous, in a sense, to take to the world and to worlds beyond. Think of the wondrous glory of giving to everyone you know an understanding of karma and reincarnation. Is this not a joy of joys?"[2]

Annice started work on two more books of her own writings, *Secrets of Prosperity* and *Memories of Mark*. She felt driven to write each of them, and many felt she was overshadowed by the ascended masters in doing so. They convey the unmistakable flame of the Brotherhood and make enjoyable reading.

Having completed her three books, in 1999 Annice turned her attention to some of Mother's publication projects. Foremost of these was the Climb the Highest Mountain series. Annice had worked with Mark and Mother on this project from 1970 to 1972 (when the first book in the series was published, containing the first seven chapters) and also in late 1970s and early 1980s when Mother had worked on additional chapters. Mother retired in 1999, and from that year to 2008 Annice completed the eight remaining volumes in the series as well as two volumes of additional material, *The Masters and Their Retreats* and *Predict Your Future,* which contains the teaching on charting your initiations in life through the science of the cosmic clock.

Mother had often spoken of the importance of the teachings in the Climb the Highest Mountain series. The masters had referred to it as the scripture for the Aquarian age, the Everlasting Gospel referred to in Revelation 14. As Annice worked on completing this key element of the mission of the messengers, she felt that this was one of the reasons she was

Annice with Mother at Annice's eightieth birthday
celebration—the last picture of the chela with her Guru.

At the Minneapolis Teaching Center in 2000.
Even after she moved to Montana, Annice frequently
returned to the Twin Cities to deliver a lecture, to counsel
and to meet with the members of the center.

sent back into embodiment after her heart attack.

Annice's retirement was hardly that of a lady of leisure. Yet she was a great example of balance in life. She was well known for her afternoon naps. When she and her body had had enough, many a meeting would end with the words, "Nap time." She knew when her body needed rest, and we all knew not to disturb her between 1:30 and 4 P.M. except in an emergency. She often slept, but sometimes just laid on her bed and rested. Her body needed the time-out.

Annice did all her work without a computer or access to email. We tried in vain to interest her in the wonders of technology, but she steadfastly refused to get a computer or learn how to use one. She appreciated all that the Internet and modern technology could do for the spreading of the teachings and enthusiastically encouraged us to pursue this avenue of contact with the world, but she knew it wasn't for her.

Friends and co-workers printed out important email messages to keep Annice in the loop, but I do not think she ever totally trusted computers. She felt that there was something about her aura that wasn't compatible with them—they just would not work for her. And who knows? She may have been right. So till the end of her working life Annice used the reliable manual methods she was familiar with, while her assistants used computers to bring the fruits of her labor to the rest of the world.

Mother had told Annice after her heart attack in 1988 that she had balanced only 43 percent of her karma at that time. This was a bit of a shock for Annice. If she had passed at that time, since she had not balanced 51 percent of her karma, she would not have qualified for her ascension. She took this very seriously, and from that time on she gave an hour of violet flame each day as often as she could to transmute her remaining karma.

She evidently made much progress, for in 1997 El Morya told her, "Beloved Annice, Serapis Bey is standing behind you, his perpetual presence over you. You have recently balanced 51 percent of your karma, and that figure very recently jumped to 61 percent."

In 2007 Annice had a serious stroke, which affected her ability to speak coherently. (The medical term for this is aphasia.) She had thought that her time might be near, and when she first learned she had had a stroke, she expected that Lanello would shortly come and whisk her off to heaven. When that did not happen, she knew that there must be some reason God wanted her to stay on earth a little longer, and she accepted the limitations that came with this new assignment. She sat up in her hospital bed laughing at her own funny speech and the jumble of nonsensical words that came out of her mouth.

After her stroke, Annice was no longer able to give her mantras and decrees. She looked sadly at me and indicated that she could no longer get the words out. Seeing Annice in this situation gave me a new appreciation of the concept, "Work while you have the light." Her many years of service and giving violet flame decrees would have to provide the momentum to see her through this next phase of her life.

Annice often used to remind us that Archangel Michael once asked the students of the ascended masters to try to live to ninety-nine years of age. At the age of eighty-four, she would often say, "I'm trying." In later years she would comment that old age is not for the faint of heart. It takes courage to go through the challenges of life's later years, especially when the body is not behaving as well as it used to.

For as long as I have known her, Annice has been dealing with various challenges to her health: a heart condition, high cholesterol, hypertension, myasthenia gravis and a thyroid condition, to name a few. But she never seemed to let these things stand in the way of her service. She had a philosophical attitude, seeing them as a means to balance karma. "I must have been naughty on Atlantis," she would say with some amusement.

She has always worked hard to maintain her health and stay in embodiment as long as she can. Along with her medications, she takes a number of natural remedies and supplements, including red yeast rice for lowering cholesterol and Hawthorne berry for her heart. God has a plan for each of us, and we must strive to live as best we can until it is time for us to go— on his timetable, not ours.

As of the time of this writing, Annice is still with us. She doesn't have the stamina of earlier years. Her words still come out wrong, but she continues to work on her speech therapy. She keeps up with the news and world events, and although she can no longer decree, she prays in her own way.

And always the chela, at the age of eighty-nine she is still working on balancing her remaining karma and looking for ways to serve the masters and their mission.

A photograph of Annice in her earlier years. I like to think of this as how she might appear after her ascension.

CHAPTER 3

Lessons in Chelaship

The following episodes from Annice's life are printed much as she told them to me. I have added my own comments, sometimes giving some of the background to the events Annice described, sometimes sharing what I learned from it.

Each story illustrates one or more spiritual principles of the Guru-chela relationship between Annice and her teachers, Mark, Mother, Serapis Bey and Morya. Her reactions, good or bad, appropriate or inappropriate, show a living, breathing and loving relationship with her teachers. One important thing to note is that she was not perfect (and she would have been the first to admit it) but she was always striving and seeking to make progress on the Path.

There is much here for each of us to learn. In the final analysis it is the quality of the heart and the striving of the soul that are important. The masters do not expect their students to be humanly perfect, like robots or machines. They understand what it is like to occupy a physical body and to be subject to the limitations of the flesh and the human consciousness. They do expect us to strive, to do our best, to try to understand why we make mistakes, and to learn from those mistakes. And when we do make a mistake, we have to pick ourselves up, balance the karma of that mistake, and move on.

Annice's life and example show certain qualities of her soul as recognizable traits from beginning to end. Her friends will remember those qualities, and I hope that they will also smile and say, "Yes, that is the Annice that I knew."

No doubt you will have your own insights as you read each story. Ask your higher self to guide you and reveal the specific lesson that may be there for you.

In this chapter, Annice's stories are set in **bold** type, my comments in normal type.

The First Time
I Met Mark Prophet

What would it be like to meet your Guru for the first time? One thing about the Guru is that he is always unpredictable. Certainly, Annice could not have predicted what would happen when she first met Mark Prophet.

Having felt the unmistakable call of the Master Jesus, she traveled to Colorado Springs to attend her first Summit Lighthouse conference. The headquarters at that time was at La Tourelle, an imposing mansion near the famous Broadmoor Hotel.

I first saw Mark Prophet at the October Class at La Tourelle in 1966. The day before the class there was a 5 P.M. Vespers service led by Mother. Mark came at the end to give the benediction, and following the service, the two of them stood at the front door shaking hands with people as they left. As Mark grabbed my hand, my knees buckled and I had to grab the door handle to save myself from falling.

Mark said to me, "You're finally here!"

I had no idea what he meant.

Lester asked if he could take the messengers to dinner. He had expected just Mark and Elizabeth but there was a van full of people. Mark said, "You don't mind, do you?"

Well, what can you say? Included in the party were staff members Ruth Jones (who has since made her ascension), Tom Miller, Bill Harper and the two children Mark and Mother had at that time.

At that dinner I had my first conversation with Mark Prophet. He said to me, "What exactly is your name on your name tag?"

"Annice," I said.

"It's the wrong name for you."

"It's the name my mother gave me."

"Well, she made a mistake!"

I thought to myself, "Who is this guy?"

"Do you know how she decided on the name?"

"Yes. She read a French novel and thought that it was the most beautiful name she had ever heard."

"Well, it is not your name. The vibration is all wrong."

Mark continued, "Do you have any sisters?"

"Yes. Doris."

"Yep, your mother made a mistake. That should have been your name."

As I thought about it in later years, the name Doris is very close to Dorcas, the name given to me by Saint Germain. So perhaps Doris should have been my given name.

From that day forward Mark called me Mrs. Booth.

What a significant first encounter. Why did Annice's knees buckle when she met the Guru? We can speculate that it was the light of the encounter with the messenger. Of course, we do not know for sure, but one thing is certain: her teacher recognized her and had been waiting for her arrival. Annice did not know what he meant at the time, but her knees gave her away. She later understood.

The touch of the Guru is significant in one's life. In the eastern tradition to make any connection with the Guru—through the touch of his hand, even seeing him or hearing his voice or remembering him—is believed to lead the soul to enlightenment.

There are still a few people in our movement who shook Mark Prophet's hand. Chances are you, the reader, were not one of them. I wasn't. But just because you never shook Mark Prophet's hand in this life, it doesn't mean that you cannot shake Lanello's hand or shake Mother's hand for that matter. Those who never met Mark or Mother physically can still make that sure inner connection with the Guru.

One way is to hear and see them through the marvelous technology of the modern world sponsored by the Ascended Master Saint Germain. We are blessed to have so many audio and video recordings of the messengers and the Teachings of the Ascended Masters delivered through them. We can see and hear them every day, if we want to, and many people do just that.

You can also meet the masters and the messengers in their etheric retreats, as you travel to those Universities of the Spirit in your finer bodies while your physical body sleeps. There are classes and conferences to attend, there is spiritual work to be done and teaching to receive to help you on your path.

You can place your hand in the hand of Lanello and Mother as your Gurus and never let go. And they have promised to place your hand in the hand of your own Holy Christ Self. How much the masters and the messengers love each one of their chelas, and how they long to take them by the hand to help them to arrive at their goal: the reunion with

God in the ritual of the ascension at the conclusion of a life of love and service.

How long has the master been waiting for your arrival at the door of his retreat? How long has he been waiting to take your hand and say, "You're finally here"?

Lanello is our ever-present Guru, so known because he is always with his chelas and letting them know that he is there for them. A simple call will suffice. Lanello says:

> It is my desire, and it is a great desire, that you accept me as being "physically" present with you. I am so near to you. If you will only incline your ear, you will hear me speaking to you through your Holy Christ Self with correct discretion and judgment and direction.... I can do, oh, so much more for you, for I have that dispensation, being the co-founder with beloved El Morya of The Summit Lighthouse. Being now a co-Guru with him and serving under him, I can do so much, beloved.... Don't forget to call to me. Lanello is my name.[3]

One insight we can glean from this story is that our name is a key to our identity. It is intended to carry the light and vibration of who we are. It is interesting to see that Mark Prophet tells Annice in their very first conversation that her name is not the one that she was intended to have. It seems that he is literally challenging who she is—or rather, who she thinks that she is. Mark was establishing her true identity and name, right from the beginning of their relationship—so much so that he no longer called her by her given name.

The Orange Dress

The day of that dinner with the messengers, I had turned up at the conference in a very smart, up-to-the-minute orange dress. I loved that dress. I had just purchased it for what was quite a bit of money for those days. I thought I looked so wonderful.

After the service Mother approached me and said, "Dear, I don't know if you know about our teachings on colors. We wear the colors of the day or white."

Mother suggested that I wear white or blue or other colors of the seven rays. I told her that these colors were not fashionable at the time.

Lester and I stopped by our motel after dinner and I said to him, "I don't think she liked my dress." So I searched through the clothes I had brought with me to find something else I could wear that would look nice. That evening, during the Holy Communion service, I was in brown and Lester was in black. Everyone else was wearing white.

I was brand new and I thought that people really did not know how to dress in The Summit Lighthouse. Not long after that, the messenger gave a teaching on wearing the colors of the days. After that lecture I wore the color of the day all through my life.

This story illustrates in an amusing way the first step on the path for many people—that our own self-assessment of who and what we are may be lacking. Annice thought she looked "so wonderful" in her orange dress, and perhaps she did by the standards of the world. But for the spiritual seeker, there is a higher standard and a higher calling. Not knowing what that higher standard is—much less how to reach it—we come to the realization that we need a teacher.

This is a test before we can even begin the path. It is often a test of the ego. Are we willing to admit that we don't know? Are we willing to admit that our cherished ideas and concepts might be wrong, or at least inadequate?

The Guru challenged her right away. Fortunately, Annice did not take offense. More important than color of her dress was the state of her consciousness. She was willing to listen and to change. Thus she could begin to walk the path of chelaship.

The ascended masters' teachings provide an interesting perspective on color and vibration. Physically, each color represents a certain band of frequencies in the electromagnetic spectrum. But more than this, each color conveys a unique vibration spiritually.

The masters encourage us to meditate on and to wear the pure colors of the seven rays, which correspond to seven different aspects of the Christ consciousness. Blue is the first ray of power, protection and good will; yellow, the second ray of wisdom and illumination; pink, the third ray of love, art and beauty; white, the fourth ray of purity, harmony and discipline; green, the fifth ray of healing and abundance; purple and gold with flecks of ruby, the sixth ray of peace and brotherhood; and violet, the seventh ray of freedom and transmutation.

By wearing these colors and having them in our environment, we can attract these qualities to us and help to magnify them in our aura. Colors to avoid are black, red and orange, which can attract and magnify negative energies. Some psychologists study the effect of color on people's emotions and even their physiology. The masters' teachings add a spiritual dimension to this study.

Annice diligently and obediently applied this teaching, and as soon as she heard Mother's lecture about the spiritual significance of color, she changed her wardrobe. All her life since that time she has worn the color of the day as each of the seven rays is more to the fore on a particular day. If you forgot what day of the week it was, all you had to do was look at Annice—pink on Monday, blue on Tuesday, Green on Wednesday, purple and gold on Thursday, white on Friday, violet on Saturday, and yellow on Sunday.

In earlier years, Mother and many of the staff at headquarters and teaching centers were quite diligent in wearing the color of the day. In later years, Mother would often wear something different, perhaps based on what she or the masters felt would best help in her assignments for that day.

Annice, however, never changed her practice. I see it as a quality of her fourth-ray sense of order and discipline. There is also a certain element of ritual in it, as each day, even for a few moments while dressing, she had the opportunity to meditate on one of the seven rays, and as the cycles of the weeks turned, to develop a balance of momentum on each of them.

The teaching on color is a useful tool on the path, but we are not rigid about it. None of us would want to make someone who has just walked in the door of our home or center feel uncomfortable about their choice of clothing or colors. Most people find out this teaching over time as they come across elements of it in our publications or observe that many who are associated with these teachings choose to wear particular colors. Or they may discover for themselves how certain colors make them feel.

Getting back to Annice's story, this situation was clearly embarrassing for her. She thought she looked so nice, and yet here was the messenger pointing out a fashion faux pas. You can imagine how upsetting such a simple thing as this might be—she has a lovely new dress that she has just purchased and really loves, and now she can't wear it.

Mother was tactful with Annice, but not really concerned about pleasing her ego. This was a seemingly insignificant episode, but like many things in life, it was a test—one that came very early in her association with the messengers. How would Annice react? Would she take offense? Would she be able to surrender a favorite dress if the teacher requested this?

Mother faced an interesting test around choice of colors early in her training as a messenger. She went to the movies with Mark and chose to wear a red dress that she had bought before she had found the teachings. The color red has a vibration that ties into anger and the forces of darkness that go with it. Mark had suggested she not wear it, but she decided to wear it anyway. She had loved that dress.

During the movie, sitting in the darkened theater, Mother felt a dark presence, an entity, sitting on her shoulder and attaching itself to her neck. She asked Mark to help her get this entity off her, but he explained that he was not able to do so since she had done what he told her not to do. So Mother had to wrestle with this force and get rid of it herself. It took her a number of days to finally deal with it.

This was a valuable lesson learned early in Mother's training to be a messenger. The masters allowed her to see and feel the effects of color on her aura and being. They respected her free will and she also had to deal with the consequences of her decision. But even more than a lesson about color, this incident was about a state of consciousness that could allow her to be disobedient to the instruction of the Guru, as Mark had that role in her life. The color of a dress may have seemed like a small thing at the time, but what a price we might pay when we are disobedient to the Guru, even in a small thing, and thereby put ourselves outside of his protection. Perhaps this experience is one reason why Mother was so careful about color and so diligent in passing on this teaching.

In later years, when Mother was asked by her chelas for guidelines about the colors they should wear, she explained that if your employment required you to wear black as a part of your uniform (for example, a waiter) then you should wear black in respect to your employer and your job. Men could wear black suits for professional reasons or if their jobs required it, but if possible, everything from the heart chakra up, including shirts and ties, should be ascended master colors. Navy blue is a good alternative to black for men's clothing.

El Morya recommended that his chelas not wear black shoes. Brown is an acceptable alternative, as it does not interfere with the flow of light in the spiritual centers in the feet. Women have a much wider range of shoe colors available, so it is less of an issue for them.

Did the messenger always wear ascended master colors? We recall seeing her in later years on occasions wearing olive green or a muted orange shade. She did not explain why she was wearing these colors. Annice said that Mother often said to her, "My initiations are not your initiations."

Trying to Meditate

After I came back home from my first Summit Lighthouse conference, I came across a book by Alice Bailey, published by an organization called the Lucis Trust. The book mentioned the names of some of the masters I had heard about through the Summit. So I said to myself, "Great, this is a book about our ascended masters."

I did not realize at the time that Alice Bailey, although she had been in training with the masters at one time, had lost her sponsorship and was not representing the ascended masters. On the back of the book it said, "Join this meditation group." I thought, "How wonderful. I don't know how to meditate, and this group will show me how." So I wrote and signed up with them to join their group. They asked on the application to send in a photograph, so I did. (Mark told me later that they could see my aura in the photograph.)

In the meantime I went back to the bookstore where I bought the book and purchased the whole Alice Bailey series at a reduced price.

Soon I received a special delivery letter saying, "We are pleased to have you as a part of our meditation group." The first lesson taught you how to meditate at the full moon. I thought it was great that I would learn to meditate at last.

You also had to send in a questionnaire each month. One

question said, "In your meditation, have you found any other groups of students of the ascended masters?"

I wrote back and said, "I don't know how to meditate, but in one of your books on such and such a page, it says that in the last quarter of the century, in the southwest of the United States, there would be a new group of ascended master students. Well, I have found it. I did not have to meditate to find it. I have found The Summit Lighthouse and the messengers Mark and Elizabeth Clare Prophet. They are in Colorado Springs, as predicted by the masters!"

Well, I got an airmail, special delivery letter back very quickly that said, "For the benefit of your soul and our group, you should be dismissed immediately. We'll pray for your soul that you will not fall into the psychic." It was signed the Lucis Trust.

I never did learn to meditate with them.

When I told Mark about this, he said, "The master saved you, didn't he? You had better not read the books that you have. To be safe, put them in my library." And so I did.

Florence Miller [another long-time student of the masters] also had some problems with the Lucis Trust. She had been in this group before joining The Summit Lighthouse. Then her parents had written to the Lucis Trust to tell them that she had joined the Summit, and they set up a prayer group to work against us.

This is a typical test that comes to a new student on the path. Often just before or just after finding the teachings of the masters, an alternative will present itself and the student will have to make a choice.

This choice becomes a test for the student—of motive, of

discernment, or some other element of consciousness. Sometimes the alternative presents itself with flattery or the promise of great knowledge or spiritual powers—or perhaps a seemingly more "friendly" atmosphere. What will the student choose? What are his priorities?

One good benchmark for discerning the true teacher from the false is something that Annice said on a number of occasions, "The false hierarchy flatters you. The real masters don't."

Sometimes the alternative that presents itself is the very same false teaching that lured us away from the path lifetimes ago. So we are faced with the same test again. And hopefully we will have learned enough, in all those years outside the mystery school, to see through the counterfeit way and no longer be lured by its attractions.

These tests can be subtle. We might wonder why they should come so early on the path. How can the student know what is the right choice before even having a chance to study the teachings and to learn the principles of cosmic law?

I think of the statement in the Bible that God will not give us a test that we are not able to pass. And perhaps this test is not so much about knowledge of the law as of motive and purity of intent. If the student is sincere and really wants to know, if he is totally honest in his motives, if he asks God to show him the way to go and *really* wants to know, if he is prepared to accept God's answer, no matter what it is, then he can make the right choice.

In Annice's case, it seems to have been a bit easier than this. The Lucis Trust threw her out before she even had to make a choice. Perhaps it was good karma of service to the masters in the past that enabled them to step in and "save" her, as Mark explained.

The messengers recommend that the masters' students not read the books by Alice Bailey, as they are not sponsored by the ascended masters and contain significant errors. They also do not recommend meditating on the full moon, since the full moon tends to amplify the negative emotional energies of the planet. Like Mother Mary, we seek to put the energies of the moon beneath our feet.

A Message from the Master

The first time I received a message from Morya, I was still in business in California. My husband, Lester, and I took Mark Prophet out for lunch. We were brand new and I was attending my second conference [the Class of Malta, held in San Francisco, October 1966]. At lunch Lester said that he'd like a glass of tomato juice, and I said, "I'll have one too."

Mark said, "No. Morya says that Annice should have pineapple juice."

I was flabbergasted. I said, "Mark, why would Morya say that to me?"

Mark said, "I don't know, but he did."

Out in the parking lot I said to Lester, "Did you realize that Morya was talking to me?" Quickly looking around, thinking that he had missed seeing the master, Lester said, "Where? Where?" He had totally missed that the master had spoken to me through Mark.

Looking back on it, I think that Morya knew about my family history of heart problems and probably wanted me to have the potassium in the pineapple juice.

Annice found it interesting that the first direct word she received from Morya through Mark was not the kind of comment one might expect. Chelas sometimes think that on meeting the master he should say something profound, something of deep spiritual significance, or give some direction for their life's work or divine plan. And perhaps the masters do this for some chelas.

But Morya's first comment to Annice was grounded in the practicalities of life. It had to do with what she put into her mouth.

In later years, serious health problems threatened to curtail Annice's lifespan and service, and looking back we can see why the master was concerned with her health. Each of us needs to live as long as we can on this earth in order to balance as much karma as we can and qualify for our ascension. And if we pass prematurely, without having balanced the necessary 51 percent, we will have to come back and start over in another body.

El Morya was lovingly caring for his student and concerned about those things which might shorten or prolong her life. It was a pattern that was to be repeated. Annice said that Morya took an interest in her health for a long time through Mark.

Here is another example:

We had just returned from India and we were all exhausted. It had been a difficult trip and we had bumped into some intense karmic records. I was a member of the staff, and Mark said, "Mrs. Booth, how do you feel?"

"Mark, I feel dirty." That was the only way that I could describe it. Just dirty.

Mark said, "Morya says you need flax."

"What in the world is flax?"

Mark said, "I don't know, but Morya says you need flax."

I talked to a staff member who had owned a macrobiotic restaurant, and I asked him, "How do I eat flax?" Stanley told me about flax seeds and how to grind them and take them each morning with cereal.

We got some flax seeds and I had them every morning on my cereal. Now, thirty years later, I'm still taking flax seed.

It was amazing how down-to-earth the master was. It was not "Oh, you wonderful chela! How fantastic you are and what a great job you are doing." Rather I got a lot of teaching from Morya through Mark which was very specific and practical instruction for me at the time. I am so grateful for it.

Annice was impressed that Morya knew about the health benefits of flax seed long before it became popular with those interested in healthy living and natural foods. In the years since Morya's direction to Annice, flax has been found to contain high levels of lignans and omega-3 fatty acids and has been shown to be useful in the prevention of heart disease and cancer.

Annice often said, "I have quite a bit of obedience built in me." If the master told her to take flax seed, she was obedient and took it. She did not stop and did not need to be told a second time.

The Eyes of Morya

In 1966 and 1967 my husband and I would travel to Colorado Springs every three months to attend the quarterly conferences, returning to our business in California after each class. I was very happy to attend classes and to be Mrs. Booth when I returned home where I was owner of the studio. When I was back home I preferred not to let anyone know that I belonged to this unusual organization.

During my second conference, Mark and Mother told me, "Morya wants you to be in charge of the San Francisco Study Group."

I was still new and did not know that there were study groups or that there was one in San Francisco. I told the messengers, "I could not possibly leave the business. And also, we are coming up to Christmas and this is the busiest time of the year for our business."

Mark said nothing, and I thought that it was the end of the conversation.

Over the next few weeks Mark sent me every piece of literature that The Summit Lighthouse had produced which had a picture of Morya in it. It got so that I was afraid to open my mail, for every time I would find Morya's eyes staring at me.

This went on for several weeks. There was never any note of explanation or letter from Mark, just a piece of literature

The Ascended Master El Morya

with Morya's picture in it, and often on the front cover. I would hurriedly put these items in the drawer beside my desk. Later I would open the drawer for some reason, and there would be Morya's eyes staring up at me! And this was in the days of the un-retouched picture of Morya, where the eyes were even more penetrating than they are today.

Finally one day I opened my mail, and there was an 8 x 10 picture of Morya. That did it! I collapsed, or rather I caved in. I called Mark and said, "All right, I surrender."

Mark said, "Oh ho! Morya's eyes got to you, didn't they? I thought that it would work." Then he hung up. And that was the extent of the conversation.

No one really knows Mark Prophet unless they worked

with him. He really is a Zen master, like his own master, Morya.

Well, once again nothing more was said about my being in charge of the San Francisco Study Group, and as time passed I thought that I was off the hook. Weeks came and went and no one mentioned it, and I certainly didn't bring it up. Then we came to La Tourelle to attend the next quarterly conference, and on the last day of the class, Mark and Mother called me into his office.

Mother said, "Annice, it is after Christmas now. How soon are you going to start the study group in San Francisco?"

I said, "I don't know anything about anything. I don't know how to run a study group. If I were to lead the decree to Astrea and someone would ask me who Astrea is, I could not answer."

Mother reached behind Mark's desk and pulled out a copy of a book with a yellow cover, *The Law of Life*, by A.D.K. Luk.* "This book tells about the masters. Each week decide which decrees you are going to give in the service and look up in the book every one of the masters listed in the preamble. No problem."

So I became the leader of the San Francisco Study Group. There were about eight little old ladies there who had decreed together for years. I had them teach me how to lead decrees and how to lead a service. Thankfully these days most people do not have to go through all that to become decree leaders or study group leaders. We have manuals that I published when

---

* We now recommend *The Masters and Their Retreats*, by Mark L. Prophet and Elizabeth Clare Prophet. This book is far more comprehensive and complete than the book by A.D.K. Luk and corrects a number of inaccuracies in the earlier work.

I became director of the Office of Ministry. They tell you exactly how to conduct services and how to lead decrees and how to conduct a study group.

To some people, Mark's methods in convincing Annice to start this group might seem unusual, or even manipulative. He used his knowledge of Annice's soul and her psychology to reach her and to persuade her to fulfill the master's direction. However, he didn't have any personal agenda. He was acting to bring about the will of God in the fastest possible way for the greatest good.

Annice herself often used psychology to entice or urge others to do what needed to be done. She used to say, "All that I know about psychology, I did not learn at school!" A student of human nature, she knew how to appeal to the highest good in others and how to encourage others to work for her or with her on a worthy project.

Sometimes people think that Annice had great training to do what she did for the messengers and their organization. Well, she did have great training, but most of it was on the job. She learned by doing the work. Annice was aware of her limitations, but she knew that a job needed to be done for the masters and she did not have to be perfect to do it. She was also humble enough to ask others to help her.

The same lesson can apply to each of us today. What assignment are you resisting that the master wants you to do for him? Perhaps he needs a study group started in your city, or perhaps he needs you to step up to the plate to lead a service or a decree session.

Are you feeling perhaps that you have not been trained or are not worthy? Or that someone else could do better than you?

Remember the example of Annice. Find out what you need to know, read the manuals, ask for help from others, and simply turn up and do the best that you can. The masters appreciate all that we are willing to do, and they do not expect us to be perfect. We can all enter in to the process of being trained as chelas if we make a commitment to that path. And much of that training is on-the-job training, as it was with Annice. We receive our training while we are engaged in the work of the master.

The Great Divine Director
and the Elementals

After the October 1966 class I went home and one month later the Class of Malta was conducted in San Francisco and Los Angeles. There were actually two classes. Lester and I went to the one in San Francisco and I will never forget it.

When I came home from the class I was working in my studio putting wedding pictures in an album, wishing that I could be there for the class in Los Angeles. The class had started that day and I could feel it. I was making a big mess, getting the photographs out of order, dropping them on the floor, curling the pictures. I was just making a mess of that album.

Finally I turned to Lester and said, "I can't stand this. I am going to get on a plane. It only costs twenty dollars and I am no good here." Lester said, "Well, I'll drive down."

We arrived at the conference in Los Angeles in the evening, and the Great Divine Director* was dictating. He was releasing the elementals. They had been very obedient to mankind's negative karma and they no longer had to stand for it.

They were to be released at midnight and the masters could not guarantee what would happen. They hoped that

---

* The Great Divine Director is a cosmic being who is the teacher of El Morya.

nothing would happen but they could not be sure.

The following day was the final day of the class. The last dictation finished at about 10 P.M., and after the dictation, as we shook hands with Mark at the door, he said to Lester, "Les, get out of town. Don't stay here. I don't know what might happen. The elementals have been given their freedom, so get as far away as possible tonight before stopping."

I did not understand this at the time. It was our first brush with karmic law and the outplaying of karma.

The final day of the Class of Malta was November 6, 1966. The following day there were two F2 tornados in Los Angeles County. The Great Divine Director said in this dictation:

> Conditions in the world today have reached a point where the Karmic Board has withdrawn all restraint from the beings of the elements. This means that the mankind of earth today do not know from one minute to the next just what the elementals will do....
>
> Inasmuch as there remains one shred of hope for mankind, [it is] that when the forces of elemental life are unleashed, and when certain destructive elements in mankind are released and unleashed without restraint, that mankind may then awaken and decide for themselves that they will cancel out the product of their own corrupted imaginations....
>
> Therefore, we sound forth tonight the edict that unless mankind shall change and correct and mend some of the terrible flaws now existent in society, certainly the elementals will be unable to hold back the tide of human creation which now stands behind

them, held in the name of cosmic mercy. Do not be surprised nor affrighted by that which comes forth, then, upon the earth; and if you wish to give your energies to try to stop it, that is your privilege. But I think that what the Karmic Board would like to have you do shall now be made known to you.

We desire that those who have formerly given their energies for the protection of mankind and for the holding back of cataclysmic action shall now turn their total attention upon the masquerades which mankind have put around themselves, the human creation which they have builded around themselves to protect themselves against spiritual power. We desire that you shall call for the walls of Jericho of human creation to fall down. We desire that you shall call for mankind to become illumined to the spiritual power that is now rising today to great cosmic heights upon this planet and is responsible for many conditions which mankind do not understand. Because mankind are not accepting that spiritual power but are rejecting it, it is breaking out in all sorts of disturbances upon this planet....

It is not essential to stop the action of cataclysm or world disturbances; it is rather to call for an awakening of mankind.... [This] will produce, if mankind will accept it, their deliverance from the karmic retribution which otherwise will descend upon them. This is inevitable; you cannot stop it! The only way you can stop it is by mankind's acceptance of the law.[4]

An Experience
of the Holy Spirit

Before I was on staff I had been to just a couple of conferences, and I still considered myself to be brand new. I thought that everything was just wonderful.

One day I was lying in my family room on the couch looking through the glass sliding patio doors out into the beautiful backyard. There was a huge pine tree over fifty feet high. I had been reading a yogic meditation book by Patanjali. I was not a meditator, and I wasn't given to seeing things, but I thought, "Gee, this is beautiful." Then, all of a sudden the walls disappeared and I seemed to enter the tree—or did the tree enter me? Was I in the tree or was the tree in me? I could not tell.

There were no shadows, and every needle of the pine tree was shimmering. It was amazing. To this day I consider it a beautiful experience. It was the golden victorious light that cast no shadow, and along with it was a noise that I could only describe as a happy wind. I recalled the words "There is no more night here." I do not know how long this experience lasted, for there was no longer any time or space for me in that garden.

Later I told Mark about the experience, and he said to me, "That was the Holy Spirit." I never told anyone about this experience at the time, not even Lester, only Mark.

I asked Mark to tell me more. I knew that Mark had all of the gifts of the Holy Spirit, and I asked him, "Have you ever experienced the Holy Spirit?" He told me about one occasion when afterwards he had felt an actual physical pain in his solar plexus. He said, "There is a price to be paid for all of these things."

The Holy Spirit is everywhere, even in the air that we breathe. Annice experienced this directly, as she felt that oneness with this universal presence as it manifested in the pine tree outside her home. The first fruits of the Holy Spirit are the oneness, harmony and profound peace that Annice felt on that day. In her case, this happened once in her lifetime.

Sometimes people have the idea that the proof of the spiritual path is to be found in these kinds of experiences and that if they are not having these transcendent revelations, there must be something wrong. But having these experiences is not necessarily a sign of progress on the path, and not having them doesn't mean a student is not advanced or not making progress.

The false gurus of the East often lure people to follow them by demonstrating psychic phenomena or by inducing experiences that are imitations of the real thing. The true Masters warn their chelas of the dangers of seeking after psychic or spiritual phenomena. These things can be a distraction from the true work of the Path—self-transformation and God's work on earth.

Yet God does sometimes grace us with experiences of great light and beauty. These can serve as a reinforcement of our faith or a vision for the future, the goal that we strive for in our own ascension into that universal presence. But, as Mark pointed out, there is a price to be paid for these things. Part of that price is that the light brings to the surface negative elements of the lesser self that must then be surrendered.

The other price that must be paid is that the world often reacts against the light of God when it manifests in man. The Gospel of John says that "the light shineth in darkness; and the darkness comprehended it not."

The Ascended Masters' SOS

One day I told Annice about an encounter with a bear. I had been working late in my office on a Friday evening. At 8:15 P.M. I heard a strange noise outside my office window. I looked out and there was a huge black bear sitting in the tree by the window, eating the fruit on the tree. I was the only one in the building and I watched him for quite a while. He was pulling down the branches, breaking them off and stripping the branches of their fruit.

I called my husband, who was working in another part of the Inner Retreat, to tell him about the bear. I thought I would be trapped in the building all night!

Then for some inexplicable reason I decided to open the blind wider for a better look at the bear. As I did so the bear looked up and we locked eyes. He looked at me for some time and then looked away, climbed down out of the tree and walked away, despite all the uneaten fruit still on the tree.

I told the story to Annice, who said that my bear story reminded her of a time in San Francisco in 1967 when she was just starting a study group.

I was leading a session of dynamic decrees when, suddenly, a person in the congregation jumped up and said, "I know how we can save the world. We need to call to ____." He said the name of a very dark entity that I cannot even lawfully speak out loud. The person who interrupted the service was a disturbed individual who had been in and out of mental institutions in this life. Mark later told me that this poor man had been a scientist on Atlantis and he had misused energy in that lifetime. [In this case, his mental condition was a result of that karma.]

Hoping to distract him, I said to him, "Well, let's finish our decrees." After the session was over, he persisted in telling me about this being I should invoke, much to my chagrin. By this time the room was bristling with psychic energy from the entity, as the pronouncing of her name had summoned her. I was so distressed that I called Mark.

Mark soon put me straight when he said: "Now listen to me. You will meet all sorts of crazed people in this work. All you have to do is look them right in the eye, and Morya will send his ray through your eye. And then you say, 'The light of God never fails, and the beloved Mighty I AM Presence is that light!' That is the panic-button call of the Brotherhood. When you give that call, someone, somewhere in cosmos has to answer."

When working for the masters, it is not uncommon to deal with opposition of various forms. The forces of darkness on the planet are threatened by the light, and they try to disrupt the activities of the Brotherhood. Most often this comes in less overt forms, such as projections of discouragement and depression. But the dark forces sometimes work through those in embodiment who are mentally unstable. It was the same two thousand years ago, when Jesus and the apostles also had their encounters with those possessed of evil spirits.

Annice had the good sense, when faced with a situation of opposition that she did not know how to deal with, to ask Mark, and he gave her a formula to invoke the assistance of the masters on the instant.

The important thing when faced with opposition is to recognize it when it occurs and to do something about it immediately. An incident like the one Annice faced is relatively easy to spot. However, when more subtle energy comes in, it is equally important to recognize it and make the calls. Don't let negative energy sit on you. Give Mark's fiat (the SOS call), calls to Astrea or Archangel Michael, or whatever is needed to deal with it and reestablish your forcefield.

The eyes are indeed the window of the soul. The messenger has since given the teaching that it may be preferable to look at the third eye or the space between the eyes at the brow rather than look directly into the eyes of someone who is mentally disturbed, and thus risk taking in their energy. There are some people you don't want to look in the eye.

"Waves Upon the Sea"

After Annice came out of retirement, she taught a class at Summit University in July 2004 and did a book signing afterwards. After lecturing for hours, signing so many books and talking to so many people, her voice gave out. She simply couldn't do any more.

This reminded her of an experience with Mark at the Easter conference in 1967. In those days Mark used to deliver nearly all the lectures and dictations at the conferences. It was the last evening of the class. He had been on the platform morning, afternoon and evening for four days. In between, he would talk to people over lunch or meet with them for counseling.

Jesus was scheduled to deliver a dictation. Mark would usually deliver a sermon or short lecture prior to a dictation, but he was so spent after four days that he decided to just go straight into the dictation. He simply didn't have the energy to deliver a lecture as well. Then he found out that some new people had arrived that evening.

I remember a time when Mark could not go on. He was so tired, and yet there were some people there who had wanted to see him and hear from him for the first time. Mark said he didn't know if he could do it. But Morya said, "We will help you."

Mark asked me afterwards how I had liked the lecture. I told him that it seemed more like a dictation than a lecture. I had started writing notes and then stopped because it seemed like a dictation. Mark then told me the story of how he had just been so tired, but the seven chohans came and delivered the lecture through him.

This lecture from the seven chohans was called "Waves Upon the Sea." It is twenty-three minutes long and is published in the album *Discourses on Cosmic Law 3*. It is the perfect lecture for a new student.

Sometimes the masters can most easily act through us when we are weakest in the human sense. Perhaps it is in those circumstances that we are most easily able to let go of the sense that we are performing some work for the masters through our human strength.

Paul spoke of this in his second epistle to the Corinthians:

> And he said unto me, My grace is sufficient for thee: for my strength is made perfect in weakness. Most gladly therefore will I rather glory in my infirmities, that the power of Christ may rest upon me.
>
> Therefore I take pleasure in infirmities, in reproaches, in necessities, in persecutions, in distresses for Christ's sake: for when I am weak, then am I strong.

Floating Away with Seraphic Meditations

The seraphim are an order of angels who serve on the fourth ray. They are great healers, fiery beings who, with their bodies and their wings, form concentric rings around the Great Central Sun. They absorb the light of the spiritual Sun, and "trailing clouds of glory," they deliver it to the far-flung evolutions of the universe, including those on our own planet earth.

Annice had an experience with these angels early in her time with the Summit.

My husband and I had our wedding photography business before coming into the teachings. It was a portrait studio. At my studio I had just returned from a conference and a *Pearl of Wisdom** came in the mail. It was from Serapis Bey, and the title was "Seraphic Meditations."[5] I used to have the *Pearls* delivered to my studio and I would open them along with the other mail, the bills, etc.

When I read the first words of the *Pearl*, "And I beheld the great electronic fire rings of the Central Sun ..." I just took off

---

* *Pearls of Wisdom* are weekly letters from the ascended masters to their students around the world. They have been published by The Summit Lighthouse since 1958.

into the higher octaves. It seemed as if I was no longer in my body.

The phone was ringing and I did not even notice it. My husband came into my office from his darkroom and said, "What's the matter with you?"

As far as I was concerned, nothing was the matter with me. I was in bliss. I do not think I was meditating. I had never been a meditator. I was a strict Methodist. I knew nothing about meditation or Eastern teachings or masters. Most people knew about the Buddha, but I knew nothing.

So as my husband was asking me questions I came to and heard the phone ringing. I picked up the phone and it was one of our customers. She said, "Mrs. Booth, I'd like to make an appointment to have my picture taken."

Even though I was back in my body, I was still not functioning well at all.

I was so out of it, I simply said, "We'd love to take your picture, but you will have to make an appointment."

"I know. That's why I am calling, to make an appointment."

"Well, we'd love to take your picture, but you will have to make an appointment. We work by appointment only."

"I know that. I am trying to make an appointment."

And around and around it went.

All this time, Lester was standing there, looking perplexed. Finally the customer on the other end of the line said, "Annice I don't think you are well today. I'd better call back another time." And she hung up.

I tried to tell my husband about this wonderful *Pearl of Wisdom,* but he turned on his heel and went back to his darkroom muttering, "If only she'd spend as much time on the business as she does on those teachings."

Immediately I changed my address for the *Pearls of Wisdom* and arranged for them to be delivered to my home, where I could read them undisturbed. I was not about to repeat a situation like that again. To this day, it is all that I can do to stay in my body when I hear "Seraphic Meditations."

The printed page can indeed hold light. The *Pearls of Wisdom*, the books, audiotapes and CDs of the Teachings of the Ascended Masters contain their radiation and vibration. Many have felt the light pouring off the pages of these sacred texts. Annice was responding to the light that was conveyed through the *Pearl of Wisdom* that arrived in her mailbox. In this instance it transported her to another world. Perhaps she responded this way because it contained the teaching of one of her favorite masters, Serapis Bey, and because she serves on the fourth ray.

Despite Annice's down-to-earth and practical ways, there is an etheric side to her nature. She is indeed the practical mystic. She is at home in the heaven world and could easily float off into the etheric octave if she is not tied down to a task. The messenger once told her she was more in the etheric octave than the physical world.

The Presence of Babaji

At one conference in 1967, Mark was giving a lecture when he suddenly stopped and said, "Did anyone feel anything?" Just as he spoke I felt as if my heart leaped out of my chest. Mark said, "Mrs. Booth did you feel anything?"

I said, "Yes, but I don't know what."

Mark explained that it was the master Babaji from the Himalayas greeting us.

After that incident, every few conferences Mark would stop and ask, "Did anyone feel Babaji?"

One time I was in the kitchen during a conference and I was making peanut-butter sandwiches. Out of a clear blue sky, Mark said, "Did anyone in the kitchen feel anything? I would like anyone in the kitchen who felt Babaji to come in."

I heard this over the loudspeaker that was set up in the kitchen. So obediently I came into the sanctuary wearing my apron.

Mark said, "That's fine, Mrs. Booth. You can go back to your peanut-butter sandwiches. I just wanted to know if you could feel Babaji."

So I went back to the kitchen, just fascinated that Mark had such an awareness of everything that was happening around him on the whole 360 degrees of his consciousness. Not only did he know that I had felt Babaji, but he also knew what kind of sandwiches I was making!

The Indian master Babaji is an unascended adept of the Himalayas. He focuses the light in the earth through a physical body, but is rarely seen by any who are not his disciples. His story is told in *Autobiography of a Yogi,* by Paramahansa Yogananda, who serves under the lineage of gurus who descend from Babaji.

I commented to Annice that it was interesting that Mark continued to mention Babaji to her, especially as Babaji is an unascended adept and he has great attainment in meditation. I ventured, "Perhaps you knew him in the Himalayas?" She replied:

Undoubtedly I knew him from past lives. All of us had to have been in the Himalayas at some time in the past. In this life, I knew nothing about Buddhas and meditation. I was a "down on my knees" Methodist. I think that I have been deliberately kept away from meditation or anything along those lines. This is a lifetime for me to work.

Pictures of the Masters

In 1967 after a class, Mark and Mother asked Lester and me to come to their rooms at La Tourelle. They explained that they needed to have pictures of the masters for our members to use. They had a number of pictures of various ascended masters spread out on display on the bed. These were pictures from other, earlier ascended master movements, including the Bridge to Freedom and Theosophy. Mother and Mark asked us which pictures we would choose as representative of the masters, worthy to be used as focuses of their light and presence.

I thought to myself, "You, the messengers, are asking me?" But I was obedient and I told them which ones I thought were good. Evidently my opinion matched theirs because they agreed with my assessment, saying, "That's what we thought, too."

The reason that this situation came about was that Mark and Mother had used a picture of the Great Divine Director that turned out to be of a false-hierarchy impostor of the master. They had to apologize to the members and ask them to return all the copies they had purchased.

The incident with the picture of the Great Divine Director was a lesson in humility for Mark Prophet. He explained that the picture had been used by an earlier ascended master activity that he respected, and the artist had given him permission to use it, so he just went ahead and printed it without checking with Morya. When he found out that the picture was of a false-hierarchy impostor, he had to eat humble pie and admit that he had made a mistake. He found that members did not lose faith in him because of the mistake, but rather their faith was strengthened because of his honesty in admitting it.

The meeting with Annice and Lester also shows the humility of the messengers and their respect for the opinions of others, especially those of people whom they trusted. They were always willing to ask other people's opinions and to consider other points of view. It is interesting to see that Mark and Mother asked this of Annice and Lester at a time when they had been studying the teachings for only a year.

This incident taught Annice that she had to learn to develop and rely on her own Christ attunement, rather than being overly dependent on Mark and Mother. She also had to know when to check with the messengers or the masters, and to have the humility to accept that her own attunement might not always be correct. It showed her the humility of the messengers and demonstrated that one must be willing to admit one's mistakes and correct them.

This incident also shows the importance of focuses of the masters having the right vibration. The picture purporting to be of the Great Divine Director was technically beautiful, many people liked it, and it had been used by a previous organization for some years. Yet Mark explained that it was a picture of a false hierarch and a focus of darkness. He took the canvas and held a ceremony to burn it in a bonfire.

Mother has explained that the consciousness of the artist affects what is conveyed through a work of art. In order to be a real focus for masters, the work needs to be of a vibration that the masters can fill with their light. Sometimes the master chooses to overshadow the artist and his work. Sometimes the picture is the Holy Christ Self or Higher Self of the artist. All too often the human consciousness of the artist is conveyed instead.

Even artists who have a good attunement with the masters can make a mistake. In the early years of The Summit Lighthouse, Ruth Hawkins, the twin flame of the ascended master Paul the Venetian, painted a number of portraits of ascended masters that have been sponsored by them. But she once painted a picture of Pallas Athena that missed the mark completely. Mother told her, "Ruth, this is not Pallas Athena. You have painted your Holy Christ Self."

The messengers have told us that many artists who have sought to paint a portrait of Jesus have actually painted a portrait of their own Holy Christ Self. This represented the highest vision of the Christ that they were able to aspire to, but it did not reach the level of being something that could convey the fullness of the blessing of the great master Jesus.

Over the years, many artists brought to Mother pictures that they had painted of various masters, looking for her approval. Only a very few received the blessing of the masters as a focus they could use. Mother said that she would rather see a blank wall and attune with the master directly than have a picture that was inadequate to convey the masters' vibration.

Averting an Earthquake

When I was fairly new to the San Francisco Study Group, Mark called one day in 1967 and said, "I am coming to the coast. Can I stay with you at your house? There is an earthquake scheduled in the Pacific Northwest, and the masters want to see if they can stop it through a dictation. Call the people together for a meeting."

So I called everyone and scheduled a meeting at the Marines Memorial Club. Mark came and stayed at our house. When it was time to leave for the dictation, we drove across the Bay Bridge in my Mustang convertible. Mark just loved to drive that car.

He was concerned about being late and he said, "I hope we make it in time for the dictation, because this fireball is closing in." Mark could see on the inner planes that a forcefield of energy was approaching the earth.

We went to get off the freeway at the usual exit, but I was chagrined to find that it was closed. Mark was in a hurry, and I said, "Mark, I don't know any other way to get there."

He said, "Don't worry. I'll get us there." And he drove through detours and back streets and made it to the Marines Memorial Club on time. I was astounded. I said, "How did you do it?"

Mark said, "I AM here!"

I said, "Yes, Mark, I know. But how did you do it?"

He said, "I just got out of my body and looked out over the city and I could see where to go."

When we arrived at the Marines Memorial Club there were a dozen or so people there. We introduced Mark and we sang a few songs and decreed and Mark introduced the dictation. Vaivasvata Manu dictated and the earthquake was averted.

The dictation by Vaivasvata Manu was delivered on September 21, 1967. When the masters release a dictation through a messenger, it is not just a teaching that is conveyed. There is also a great light that is released. This light can have many different kinds of actions in the earth. For example, it can bring enlightenment or healing to people, far beyond those who are in the room.

Vaivasvata Manu did not mention the projected earthquake in his dictation. Evidently it was not necessary for people to know what might have been. The masters often work in this way, not seeking outer recognition, but content to know that life has been blessed by their service.

This episode shows Mark's adeptship and attunement with the masters and also how the masters can use a relatively few people to avert a calamity. We may never know what our prayers accomplish.

Transferring Glyphs

One day in 1967 or 1968 when I was very new to the teachings and not yet on staff, Mark looked at me intently. I felt the intensity of his gaze and was concerned. I felt that something was happening, and so I said, "Mark, what are you doing? What's wrong?"

Mark said, "I am transferring glyphs into your etheric body."

Mark was evidently transferring certain inner energy patterns, called glyphs, into Annice's etheric body. He did not tell her why, but perhaps it was something that was necessary for her future work with the ascended masters. One could speculate that these glyphs, for example, enabled her to do her part in the work of completing the Climb the Highest Mountain series.

The Buddha Amitabha once described how the glyphs in the consciousness of Mark Prophet were used to deliver the prayers and dynamic decrees that form the foundation of the ascended masters' Science of the Spoken Word:

> Every now and then individuals come along and say, "We will rewrite the decrees; they do not make sense," or "We will write our own decrees, for we, too, have talent in poetry." Recognize that it is not

mere poetry that makes a decree but science and poetry and the inner engrams of the Word.

These were yet in the Causal Body and in the chakras of Mark Prophet from ancient days of Atlantis when he was a master of invocation and a priest of the sacred fire. Therefore, through these hieroglyphs and glyphs of the mind held in the aura of this saint—this very human saint who moved among you—various members of the ascended host did dictate through him the formulas for total world liberation that you now have recorded in your decree books.[6]

The masters have described glyphs of light as initiations which can be deciphered by the I AM Presence. In *The Path of the Higher Self,* chapter 7, we read about glyphs and how the ascended masters use cosmic glyphs flashed forth from the I AM Presence to transfer discoveries and inventions to mankind:

While it is true that the increase in the world's population has been facilitated by advances in science and technology, it should be understood that all of mankind's discoveries and inventions have come forth from the Lords of Karma by special dispensation and that no forward movement of the race is ever made without their approval and the assistance of the entire cosmic Hierarchy. The creative genius of man is the spark of the Christ Mind. As Jesus knew full well, it is the Father—the Spirit, the animating Principle—which quickens the lump of clay that of itself can do nothing.

Those flashes of insight which the great of all ages experience are actually cosmic glyphs flashed forth from the I AM Presence to the outer consciousness. Even the steady plodding of the empiricists and the superhuman constancy of a Copernicus, a Brahe, a Kepler, or a Galileo, who have held high the torch of civilization, are directed and empowered from above. We must remember that the miracles and blessings of science were never intended to be used to subject the flame to mechanization, but rather, by the grace of God, to free the race from the death grip of a mechanical existence in order that billions of souls might have a greater opportunity to work out their karma, gain self-mastery, and fulfill the purposes of Life.[7]

Lady Dorcas

In 1960, the ascended master Saint Germain established the Keepers of the Flame Fraternity within The Summit Lighthouse. For those who wished to dedicate themselves to his cause of keeping the flame of life for earth and her evolutions, the Master pledged his assistance and sponsorship on the path.

In the early years of the fraternity, Saint Germain from time to time held knighting ceremonies, where he recognized individual members and bestowed the title of knight or lady of the flame. Annice received this blessing from the master a little over two years after she found the teachings.

There was a time in our organization when some members of The Summit Lighthouse were initiated by Saint Germain as knights or ladies of the flame. On these occasions the master would give the student a new inner name. I was knighted by Saint Germain on July 26, 1968, through Mark Prophet. Saint Germain gave me the name Lady Dorcas.

Dorcas was a woman of the early church mentioned in the Bible in the book of Acts. She made coats and garments for others. She died and was resurrected by Peter.

The story of Dorcas' resurrection is told in Acts 9:36–42:

Now there was at Joppa a certain disciple named Tabitha, which by interpretation is called Dorcas: this woman was full of good works and almsdeeds which she did.

And it came to pass in those days, that she was sick, and died: whom when they had washed, they laid her in an upper chamber.

And forasmuch as Lydda was nigh to Joppa, and the disciples had heard that Peter was there, they sent unto him two men, desiring him that he would not delay to come to them.

Then Peter arose and went with them. When he was come, they brought him into the upper chamber: and all the widows stood by him weeping, and showing the coats and garments which Dorcas made, while she was with them.

But Peter put them all forth, and kneeled down, and prayed; and turning him to the body said, Tabitha, arise. And she opened her eyes: and when she saw Peter, she sat up.

And he gave her his hand, and lifted her up, and when he had called the saints and widows, presented her alive.

And it was known throughout all Joppa; and many believed in the Lord.

Some years later, Annice found out that she had been embodied as Dorcas.

I have a habit of being resurrected. As Dorcas I was brought back from death by Peter, the disciple of Jesus, and in this life as Annice Booth I was saved by the messengers, who resur-

rected me after the cardiac arrest following my heart attack.

I made coats in that embodiment as Dorcas, another thread which was pulled through to this life when for a period of time I was in charge of a woolen mill in Minneapolis that made beautiful garments for The Summit Lighthouse. Sometimes the themes of our lives repeat themselves.

The Spoken Word
and the Written Word

Annice began helping the messengers with their work on publications very early in her service, even before she joined their staff. In this story she recalled her first involvement with the Keepers of the Flame lessons. She started working with Mother on these lessons in 1968.

In 1968 the messengers were on the *SS Bremen* sailing to Europe, and I was on that trip. Mother asked if I would help her with her work, and I said, "Sure."

Mother said, "Well, come out on the deck." There was a desk on the deck ready for our work. We started working on Keepers of the Flame lessons. There had been twenty-six published to that point and Mother asked me to start working with her on lesson twenty-seven. She said, "Here is a dictation from Hilarion for us to edit."

I was shocked. "What do you mean, edit?"

"You silly goose. You don't think that every single word Mark says in a dictation can be printed exactly as he said it, do you?"

"Do you mean you want me to change the words of the dictation?"

I felt as if my whole world was in a shambles.

But I gradually caught on. Mother explained to me that the spoken word is different from the written word.

Mother has spoken about the process of editing the dictations and misconceptions people have about this. Sometimes they have the idea that the dictations arrive almost punctuated and paragraphed in midair. And in one sense, they may be, which is all the more reason why a high attunement is needed by those who work as editors. They have to be able to tune in to the consciousness of the master to do the work most effectively. The written word is different from the spoken word, and nuances of tone and emphasis that convey so much meaning in the spoken delivery must be translated by the editor in order to convey on the printed page the full import of the original release.

The messenger worked with her editors to accomplish this goal. Sometimes she made more extensive changes when a dictation was prepared for print. In these cases she explained that the master who delivered the original dictation would place his Presence with her and dictate what he wanted in the printed *Pearl,* which might be quite expanded from what had originally been delivered before an audience.

The Call Compels the Answer

One time on the European tour with the messengers, I was riding in the car with them. I was in the back seat and the messengers were in the front. It looked as though a storm was imminent and there was thunder and lightning.

Mark said to me, "Annice start making the call." I was quite new in the teachings at that time and I didn't know what Mark meant. I said, "What is a call, Mark?"

Mark said, "Start to decree!"

Can you imagine a messenger asking me to decree?

So I said, "What do I decree about Mark?"

Mark said, "A storm is coming and I want to get through this one-way road."

"What shall I decree?"

"Don't you know 'Clear the Way for the Children of the Light'?"

I grabbed my decree book and started to give the decree, softly and timidly. Here was the messenger in the front seat, and I was in the back seat saying the decree.

> *Clear the way for the children of the Light!* (3x)
> *Beloved I AM!*
> *Clear the way for the children of the Light!* (3x)
> *Take thy command!*
> *Clear the way for the children of the Light!* (3x)

> *Release thy power!*
> *Clear the way for the children of the Light!* (3x)
> *Enfold us each hour!*

Mark said, "Say it!"

What he meant was, "Annice, say it louder!"

I kept increasing the volume until I was roaring.

And then suddenly everything was fine. The weather cleared up, the traffic cleared and we went straight on through to our destination.

I asked Annice, "What did you learn from that experience?" She said, "I learned not to be scared to give the decrees while the messenger was present. The call is important and it doesn't have to be the messenger's call."

What a lesson. Mark was a master of invocation on Atlantis, an expert in the art of the call and the science of the spoken Word. Perhaps he could have given one fiat that could have parted the clouds and cleared the way, as he did on other occasions. But this time he asked Annice to decree. He knew that it would make an impression on her and that she would remember this lesson. At the very least Annice learned not to be self-conscious about decreeing out loud.

Mother once said, "The masters tell us, 'The call compels the answer.' It says *the* call. It does not say that it has to be *my* call." Many times people contacted the messenger to ask for her calls for themselves or for situations in the world. That is part of the work that she did—she made calls and invocations on behalf of her chelas and all mankind. But it could become a problem if people began to not make their own calls but rely on her to make the calls for them.

It was as if Mark was saying to Annice, "You can give the

call, too. You have an I AM Presence and a Holy Christ Self, and you can give a fiat as powerfully and with the same results. You can become the master. Just fulfill the requirements of the law. Be sincere and only ask for that which is lawful, adjust your calls according to God's will. Don't be timid. Put your heart into it. And for best results, give the call out loud, with full voice."

Annice's story reminded me of an experience I had with Mother in 1994. I was on the phone with her late one night, and we were working on a document, she in her office and I in mine. We had been going back and forth all day on this particular communication to the field, which had to go out the next day. This must have been our fifth or sixth detailed conversation we had about it that day. It was a stressful time and I was tired.

Mother opened the phone conversation with the statement, "I can't find my glasses. Make a call!" She needed her reading glasses to read the document I had faxed to her, and she could not find them amongst all the things on her desk.

I was taken aback. I did not expect this. The messenger cannot find her glasses and she expects me to make a call for her about such a mundane thing? Why didn't she make a call about it? Was she testing me? Of course she was. But what did it mean? All this ran through my mind in a flash.

First things first. Be obedient. I felt awkward but I made a call. In a rather soft voice I summoned my resources and said, "In the name of the Christ, beloved Cyclopea, please help Mother to find her glasses." Then Mother said, "Thanks! I found them. They were right in front of me on the desk."

It seemed to me then that she was a human being just like me. She could lose her glasses just like any one of us. She needed someone else to help her from time to time. And it did not have to be her call. Then we went right on with our work and got the job done.

It was seemingly a small thing compared with Annice's experience. But it made an impact on me and has helped me remember Mother's teaching, "It's not *my* call, but *the* call."

"It is Finished!"

In later years, as Annice was working on a publication she could often hear Mother's voice in the words on paper. On one occasion she literally heard Mother's voice speaking the words in her mind.

However, another editor was editing this particular publication for the second time. She was trying with the best of intentions to improve upon it, to perfect it to her way of thinking. But Annice felt that it was becoming a different book. It no longer sounded like Mother, it no longer had her flame or her voice. So Annice went back to the original version of the book. Here is what she told this editor:

Even after this book is printed we might find mistakes or ways that it could be improved. But there comes a time when you have to say, "It is finished!" Let me tell you my "It is finished!" story.

It was back in the days of La Tourelle and I was not even on staff yet. Mark told me to come down to the basement to see Tom Miller's latest painting. It was a mystical painting of the Christ. Tom was there with his brushes, saying, "I have to do this and touch up that and change this."

Suddenly through the very ethers came this absolute roar from Mark Prophet: "IT IS FINISHED!"

I said, "Oh! My gosh!" It scared me half to death, but I knew it was Jesus speaking through Mark.

Mark went on to say, "Alright, Tom, put your brush down. The master has said it is finished!"

Tom said, "But I want to do this and that ..."

Again Mark said, "It is finished!"

The moral of the story is that one can always go back and revise something, but there comes a certain point when you have to say, "It is finished!" and you have to know when that point is. Otherwise you can completely destroy the original release of the master and the radiation of the release and start to insert yourself in it.

Annice then said to the editor:

Now, before you do any more work on this book, go and do Astreas. Forget about reading with your head. Let your heart read the book.

The publications of The Summit Lighthouse are so unique because they contain the radiation of the master. Because of this, they change lives. The goal of the editor is to get him or herself out of the way and to not enter into the process with the human self. Ideally the Christ mind of the editor should edit the book.

The most important thing about a publication is the flame and the vibration of the messengers and the masters. The teaching it contains is vital, but it is the flame and the light that will convert a soul. This is what must come through the publication and what should radiate off the pages. It is the light that attracts the reader and speaks to the soul and heart and mind.

The other lesson from this story is Morya's concept of timing. You can work on something forever making human improvements, but if you miss the cycle for its completion the battle can be lost. You have to be able to complete a project for the masters and get it out on time. Annice was very capable of this and did it many times in her seventies and eighties.

The greatest opposition to a project is often on the 11 o'clock line. It can come through your own carnal mind, ever thinking of human improvements. We need to remember to seek to convey the flame of the Holy Spirit rather than look for outer perfection.

A Couple of Ladies in Waiting

I once saw a photograph of the staff at La Tourelle and was surprised not to see Annice in it. She groaned and said that the reason she was not in the photograph was that she and Lester had taken it. The experience had been quite an initiation.

I remember that we had such trouble taking that picture because everyone was moving around and they could not sit still. I was not in it because I was behind the camera. Besides, I was not yet on staff.

Annice knew everyone by name and could tell me all their stories. So we went through the list. They all seemed to be wearing white, and I asked if they were in uniform. She said, "No it was probably just a Friday and they wore white."

I asked Annice to tell me about the other ladies in the photo.

I was younger than most of these ladies. Most had been in the I AM movement and some had been in the Bridge to Freedom. Marguerite Baker was a teacher and it was her story that was written in the book *And then the Angels Came to the First Grade Children*.[8] Helen MacDonald wrote the book for her.

Marguerite Baker had a friend called Lorraine. Marguerite wore her hair in a beautiful white beehive hairstyle, with not a hair out of place. Her friend Lorraine would lay out her clothes for her, draw her bath and do her hair. Lorraine said that in a past life Marguerite was the queen and she had been her lady in waiting.

Mark told me that actually it was the other way around. Marguerite was the lady in waiting in that earlier life and Lorraine had been the queen, but they had switched roles in this life. That is the danger of reading the akashic records.* You can tune into the right period but the wrong record.

It is better not to dwell upon any of it. Dwell instead upon humility and being the servant of the Christ in all. I recall Mark down on his knees scrubbing the floors in all joy and humility.

The two ladies got it wrong. The one who thought she had been the queen had actually been the lady in waiting. But perhaps in another sense they got it right. It could be that they were doing what they needed to do to balance their karma and for each of them to learn to play the other role. But the moral of the story is to not take your ideas about your past lives too seriously. As Annice said, "Better not to dwell on any of it."

---

* Akasha is primary substance, the subtlest, ethereal essence, which fills the whole of space; "etheric" energy vibrating at a certain frequency so as to absorb, or record, all of the impressions of life.

A Karmic Return

Some time in 1968, or maybe it was early 1969, Mark called me on a Thursday night with a message. He said, "Morya is not sure he can hold back the elementals this weekend and he wants to be sure that you are out of town."

I said, "Well, Mark, I've got a society wedding to do." I had worked hard to get this appointment.

Mark said, "Give it to someone else, because Morya wants you out!"

By this time Lester was 100 percent in the teachings and he was obedient to the letter. We packed most of our most important things in case there was no San Francisco to come back to. We gave the society wedding to our competitors, got into our Mustang convertible, and headed for Reno, Nevada. Mark had told us to get to high ground and we did.

We parked outside a trailer park in Reno, looked at ourselves and said, "Well, so far nothing has happened." Then all of a sudden there was a horrible wind. It blew furiously and overturned three-quarters of the trailers in the trailer park. As we watched the wind, we knew it was the outplaying of returning karma. But we were unharmed.

Once it was over, we got to a phone and called Mark.

He said, "What are you doing?" We told him what had happened.

Then he said to us, "You are safe now. Go back. Morya needed a physical body through which the masters could release the energy and he wanted to be sure that your lives would be safe."

We turned around and drove back home.

This is quite a curious story. Evidently there was an accumulation of burden on the elementals that they could no longer bear, and it had to be released in some way. Annice and Lester assumed that the message meant the projected karmic return was to happen in San Francisco, but this is not how things worked out.

Mark did not give all the details of Morya's plan or explain exactly why things happened the way they did. Was the karmic return diverted to an area where it would do less damage than if it had occurred in the city of San Francisco? We do not know. In any case, Annice and Lester were obedient to the Master's request, and things evidently worked out as they were supposed to.

Sometimes the masters need to have our bodies in a certain place or to have us sleep in a certain city so they can anchor light there. On a few occasions Mark told Annice to go to a city and stay overnight. She asked him what specific calls she should make while she was there. He told her not to think about it too much. If she thought about it too much, she might interfere with what the masters were trying to accomplish.

So next time your plane is delayed, you miss a connection and you have to spend an unplanned night in a distant city, it could be opposition to your mission. Or perhaps the masters need you there for some inner work.

Joining the Messengers' Staff

While I was in Colorado Springs for the New Year's class in 1969, Mother said to me, "Have you ever done any writing? I need to get out *Climb the Highest Mountain*. Mark is insisting that we get it out soon." They had been working on it for some years and it was still not published. "If you will stay with me for three months until the next class, I know we can get this book finished."

I did not know what to say. I had been asked to come on staff several times before but my husband and I had always cited our business in California as an excuse.

Finally Mother asked Lester and me to come to her room after the conference. She told Lester, "I have got to have Annice or I am not sure I can carry on."

Lester, "Mother I want you to carry on! Of course you can have Annice."

Mother, "That means that she will be on staff."

Lester, "Fine she can be on staff in Santa Barbara."

And so I came to work on staff in 1969.

Three years later, in 1972, we finally printed that book.*

---

* Mark originally planned for *Climb the Highest Mountain* to be a single book with thirty-three chapters, but as more and more material was written, it became clear that it would need to be more than one book. The first seven chapters were published in 1972. Eight additional volumes in the series were published from 2000 to 2008, completing the thirty-three chapters.

The Master Trains Us Well

I had just joined staff at the Motherhouse and had flown to Colorado Springs two days before the Easter class to help. We were using Mother's oblong dining room table as our sales area during the conference. I was sitting there checking invoices and arranging displays. Mother came to me and said, "What's bothering you dear? I can see that something is bothering you."

I had just been thinking, "I sold my business to come on staff to serve the masters, and here I am doing exactly the same thing as I did in my own business—checking invoices and arranging displays!" So I explained this to Mother.

She said, "Yes, dear. Morya trained you well, didn't he?"

Lanello says, "Yes, beloved, your daily tasks and obligations and responsibilities have everything to do with your initiations on this staircase of life. Dispatch them well!"[9] Even our everyday mundane work has everything to do with fulfilling our mission and balancing our karma in this life.

Mother was pointing out that Morya had a hand in the kind of work that Annice had done and that he was responsible for her training, even before she contacted this activity. This work would be useful to her when later she was serving the ascended masters and their messengers. When we are on track with our inner blueprint and the path of chelaship, everything becomes a stepping-stone to our service to the masters and their mission.

Many chelas when they first came on staff were placed in positions that they had not expected. A common assignment was the kitchen, or after our headquarters moved to Montana, the farm and ranch crew. For some who had come from professional backgrounds, this required a certain humility. These were ideal places to test new chelas. They also allowed these chelas to work off some of their worldly substance, learn the basics of the path and of chelaship, and find out how to get along with other chelas.

The kitchen could be an intense place to work. It took team work, attunement and attainment to get a healthy and wholesome meal out to a hungry community on time, on budget and in the right vibration. Part of the challenge of the kitchen is that food relates to the solar-plexus chakra, so those working in the kitchen had to hold a degree of balance for the emotional bodies of all in the community.

The vibration of the food was all-important. It could affect the health, work and harmony of the whole community. Mother told the kitchen staff that in the spiritual communities of the East, it was the highest initiates who were chosen to serve in the kitchen, since their work had such an important effect on the health, both physical and spiritual, of the entire community.

Those who cooked for Mother had to be especially careful of their vibrations. They tended to be a special group. They talked very little while preparing the food and were conscious of maintaining their spiritual attunement and putting their love into all that they did.

The Masters Use
Our Adaptability

One day Annice changed the list of books that we were working on because the circumstances in the publishing department had changed. She spoke of the quality of adaptability when she explained her decision.

Mark bought the Motherhouse at Santa Barbara in 1969. My title was supposed to be "House Mother of the Motherhouse." When Mark first told me, I laughed. He said, "Don't laugh. You will find out what it means."

And I did find out. I did everything at the Motherhouse—everything except take the dictations. Spiritually, I was supposed to hold the position of the Christ in the center of the mandala. Physically, I scrubbed the floors, ordered the food, led the services, supervised the staff ("spanked" them when they needed it) and was involved in the many other facets of training chelas and running the Motherhouse. In addition I was treasurer and in charge of the finances.

All was going well. Then Mark called and said, "Elizabeth needs you back here in Colorado Springs to finish *Climb the Highest Mountain*."

My husband was in Santa Barbara, and this would be unsettling for us. I would have to go back and forth between the two locations. But I said, "Mark, I am fairly adaptable."

Mark said, "Yes, Mrs. Booth, and that adaptability is what the masters can use."

That's why I won't be bound to a book list that I wrote myself.

The messengers have told us many times that "mobility is the sign of the chela." The more adaptable and flexible we are in our consciousness, the greater use we are to the master.

Change is a given on the spiritual path. We need to change our consciousness, change our karma, change our psychology. After all, if we were already perfect, we wouldn't still be here —we would have ascended long ago.

How does the Guru help us make the necessary changes? One technique is to change our circumstances, change our assignments, change our location. When we change the outer, we have an opportunity to change the inner as well. These outer changes also encourage nonattachment to the things of this world.

The seeming changeability of the Guru was something that would occasionally upset a chela. If misunderstood one might think that the Guru was capricious, unpredictable or even erratic, but there was often a higher purpose at work. For example, the messenger would introduce rules about how she wanted a certain assignment done. Chelas might initially struggle with this, make mistakes, think they knew a better way. Eventually, they would learn the system.

And then, just when it seemed that everyone was comfortable and everything was going fine, Mother would change the rules. This might cause a certain amount of chaos and confusion, but it also meant it was not possible to take things for

The Keepers of the Flame Motherhouse in Santa Barbara

granted or perform tasks robotically and with merely an outer mastery. It was necessary to think, to strive to do better, and to endow the task with the flame of the heart.

One thing that it is important to understand about the path is that there are things which work in the Guru-chela relationship that do not work in our relationships with others —either in our private or professional lives. Sometimes even well-meaning students would see Mother acting in a certain way and decide to copy this in their interactions with co-workers or people that they supervised. But coming from the wrong vibration, this could easily turn into power plays or tyranny over others.

We cannot play the guru. If we do, we will surely come to grief. Life throws enough curve balls and unexpected circumstances for all of us to receive our tests and initiations. There is no need to deliberately try to create difficulties or tests for one another.

Morya gives some important keys to the process of initiation in chapter 15 of *The Chela and the Path*:

> We will not spoon-feed our chelas. We expect to be met at least halfway. The oatmeal is on the spoon. Let those who are hungry lean forward, take the spoon, and feed themselves! We demand the mind of the chela conform to the mind of God. Hence our method in the presentation of the law is often after the koan of the Zen masters. We allow the enigma of divine reason to challenge human reason, to force the soul to a new plane, the plane of the rationale of the eternal Logos....
>
> We do not promise to do for our chelas what they must do for themselves.

Karma with a Staff Member

One day a new student walked into the chapel at La Tourelle for the very first time. He had just found the teachings. Later Mark called me into his office and said, "Mrs. Booth, do you like this man?"

"Oh yeah, Mark. He seems real nice."

"Well, that's good, because you sure didn't like him the last time around."

Mark said, "You can go back to work now."

And that was the end of the conversation.

This man joined staff soon after this. Later, after I had found out that I had been Mary, Queen of Scots, I learned that he had been Bishop John Knox, the leader of the Scottish reformation. He had opposed the Catholic queen with his inflammatory speeches.

Mark told me, "Now you've balanced a piece of your karma." I had served harmoniously with this person I had a problem with in a previous life.

Very often the masters do bring us together with those we have the most karma with from past lives. This is especially the case for those who have made a commitment to the path and are seeking to balance their karma and make their ascension.

Our ability to work together harmoniously with people, even those we may have the most intense karma with, is a key test on the path. These kinds of karmic relationships are not uncommon, but it is not necessary to know all the details of our previous interactions, as Annice did not initially in this instance. Our commitment to the path, to maintaining our harmony, and to invoking the violet flame for the transmutation of karma can see us through.

To Sleep But Not to Dream

One day Annice wanted to go to town to do some errands, and I suggested that we get an early start. Normally I would pick her up around 10 A.M., but on this occasion she agreed to be picked up at 9. I called her at 8 to make sure that she was awake. When I called she sounded very sleepy and said, "Good heavens, it's not even light out. I am not even in my body yet. Do you always get up this early in the morning?"

When I went to pick her up she was still a little out of it. It even took her a while for her voice to warm up. And she was laughing and remembering why she did not get up this early. It simply did not work for her.

When I sleep I go somewhere far off and very deep. I don't know where I go, but it is far away.

One time Mother and I were talking about dreams. I said, "Well, Mother, I just don't dream."

Mother said to me, "No, dear, you are out of your body teaching in the retreats."

I was astounded. I was still fairly new to the teachings, and I never remembered going to the retreats. Nor did I think that I was a teacher. But I was teaching it on the inner before I knew it on the outer.

By the time we got to town, Annice was fine and ready to eat her breakfast. That was the last time that I got Annice up so early. It pained me to see her so distressed and not functioning well.

Trust No Man!

At La Tourelle in my early years on staff I was going through my naïve phase: I was being too trusting and giving people too much benefit of the doubt. I trusted everyone.

Mark said to me one day, "Morya wants me to tell you, Mrs. Booth, *Trust no man. Trust only God.*"

This was personal instruction from Morya to me privately.

It was evident that the master was taking an interest in his chela and was using his messenger to instruct her. Morya's statement was short and to the point.

Annice took the master's words to heart. The message was only two short sentences, six words. But she pondered those words and applied them to her life.

In later years no one would ever have called Annice naïve or over-trusting. But Morya perhaps could see that Annice was too trusting at this stage and that this could get her into trouble in the future. She would later work with people from study groups and teaching centers throughout the world. She would need to be a student of human nature, to develop her intuition and Christ mind and learn not to be taken in by the not-self or carnal mind of anyone. (For we all do have a not-self, the negative portion of consciousness, which is known in esoteric literature as the dweller-on-the-threshold.)

111

We have been told that the masters are able to observe their students, to see their auras and to know on an instant what they are manifesting (for good or ill) and what may be lacking. The master can intercede, especially if the chela has given decrees for the master to have the spiritual energy in reserve to use in times of trouble. In later years, Morya explained that his intercession for his chelas was on the basis of "pay as you go." We have to give him the energy he needs to be able to intercede in our lives. Therefore his chelas love to give his decree 10.03, "I AM God's Will."

Lanello explains how much it can mean for us to have the assistance of one of the ascended masters in our lives:

> Beloved ones, many of you are yet fragile. Many of you require our sustaining presence. You work hard with your decrees and in your service, but you do not have the sense of co-measurement of just how much strengthening and overshadowing you receive, not only from ourselves but from the holy angels and many ascended masters.
>
> You can consider yourselves in one sense of the word as mature sons and daughters of God with great knowledge of the Path and in another sense of the word as newly born babes yet in incubators, not able to live outside those incubators until you are strengthened.
>
> So, there is a side of the nature that is fragile, there is a side of the nature that is strong. And again, beloved, it is relative, so that you know not when you are weak and you know not when you are strong.
>
> Thus, the ascended masters do come and we do dote over you, but we do not indulge you. And we are fierce in challenging you when you allow yourselves to

express the not-self. This cannot go unnoticed. This cannot go without discipline. This deserves the cosmic spanking because all of you know better and all of you are capable of doing better.[10]

The Shrinking Baby Clothes

When Mother was young and Sean [her first child] was a baby, her aunts in Switzerland sent beautiful baby clothes—a hand knit layette with booties, caps, sweater and blanket.

She did not have a lot of funds at the time and so she was thrilled with the gift. The messengers had a very small staff and Mother's assignment from Morya was to write. The laundry was left to one of the men, who was not adept at doing laundry. The beautiful knitted wool baby clothes came out of the hot setting on the washer and dryer as a perfect set of doll clothes. Mother was absolutely shattered. She cried for days. Nothing like this had ever happened before and she was brokenhearted.

The aunts sent another set. (She had tactfully not told them what happened to the first one.) Again there was another set of doll clothes. She was devastated and cried again.

After a while, Morya said to her, "How long are you going to let this bother you? The force* knows exactly your point of vulnerability, and they will work it every time until you get over it and no longer react."

Mother decided that no matter what happened to the

---

* A shorthand term used to describe forces of darkness and false hierarchies of evil, generally fallen angels and malevolent disembodied spirits inhabiting the astral plane.

laundry, she would not get upset. She learned to not react but to make the calls on the energy. And of course, it never happened again. The aunts started knitting in nylon and acrylic, and the staff stopped throwing the baby clothes in the washing machine. As long as the force knows that we react to a point of vulnerability, they will play the same tune on the piano.

This reminds me of the story of Clovis at the time of the tribal chiefs in France. Clovis was an embodiment of Mark, and Clothilde, his wife in that life, was an embodiment of Mother, his twin flame. Clovis was the first to unify the tribes and he achieved that goal through the intercessory prayers of his wife. He promised to become a Christian if he won the battle. His wife prayed, the battle was won and all of France became Christian.

It is often the little details of life that can most upset us. I don't know why this story reminded Annice of Clovis and Clothilde. But Mother was a woman who a number of centuries ago had been a queen whose prayers were responsible for the union of France and the conversion of the nation to Christianity. In this life she had a world-wide mission for the ascended masters. Yet here she was, upset by something as mundane and inconsequential as the shrinking of her laundry.

The tests of life often come at our point of vulnerability, and the forces of darkness always seem to know what is our weakest point. The force had found out exactly how to get Mother to lose her harmony. But as soon as she decided she wasn't going to fall for the trap, it stopped happening.

The masters often teach us lessons using the simple everyday circumstances and opportunities of our lives. Sometimes we have the idea that initiations on the spiritual path should come in grand forms—battles won and dragons slain. But more often they come through our seemingly ordinary daily tasks and assignments. It is essential on the path that we pay attention to these, performing them well and to the best of our ability.

An interesting phenomenon that is illustrated in this story is that those who worked around the messenger had to be careful about their state of consciousness and the way that they performed tasks. The messenger wore an intense aura of light, and the masters used her aura to anchor light for the planet. This light often caused a reaction in those around her. It was not uncommon for normally efficient and capable people to become clumsy or somewhat incompetent in her presence as her light contacted and stirred up the density in their own aura, irritating them or making them less functional.

We need to pray for those who work with us or for us, especially if they are assisting in projects for the masters. They may be sincere and dedicated, professionals in their fields, but if they are not used to the light, it may cause a reaction. We can ask that our own light or the light of the masters does not disturb or upset them.

Saved for the Summit

I was always mystified as to why I had never found any other ascended master activities before I came to The Summit Lighthouse. When I was in college in the 1930s there was a beautiful I AM Temple in Oakland, twenty-five miles from where we lived, but I never heard of it and never attended. I never heard of the I AM activity.

I said to Mark one day, "Mark, I cannot understand why others were in the Bridge to Freedom and the I AM activity and yet I never heard of the I AM."

Mark said, "Morya had you marked for this activity. If you had been in any other there was so much inharmony and backbiting that you might have left it completely. Morya insulated you from all other groups and saved you for The Summit Lighthouse."

The ascended masters are long-range planners. They know their chelas before they enter embodiment and they lovingly nurture and care for them. The masters tell us that they choose the time when they allow their chelas to contact their outer activities. They cannot send them to a group where there is bickering and backbiting and infighting. They would rather that they stay at home and study the teachings on their own than risk losing a precious soul who might be turned away from the path for a lifetime through a bad experience with a group. So they often wait until their chelas are stronger before sending them to meet other chelas.

El Morya once told us through Mother that our victory depends on absolute harmony within our groups and within the organization as a whole. If harmony is present, then we can and will magnetize many wonderful souls of light who are looking for these teachings. But we can actually prevent the success of the ascended masters' activities if we allow inharmony, jealousy or vying for power to manifest. Even petty dislikes between members can affect the success of the group.

So what can we do if we have karma with other people in a group? What can we do if we have difficulty maintaining our harmony with another?

The solution is to place our attention on and speak to the Holy Christ Self of the other person. When we place our attention upon the heart of another and remind ourselves that God lives in that heart, we can be healed in a deep and profound way and we will see the greatness in another chela.

This concept gives a new insight into Jesus' teaching, "Inasmuch as ye have done it unto one of the least of these my brethren, ye have done it unto me."[11]

The Burning Candle

I had just bought some candles. I knew that Annice rarely used candles and I wondered why. Annice said, "Get out your pad of paper and let me tell you about my candle story with Mother."

Mother always had a candle burning on the table at which she worked. One day Mother and I were in the Tower at La Tourelle. She had a 48-hour candle burning, which had been a Christmas gift. It was four inches square and eight inches tall.

Mother and I were called away from our work and we left the candle burning, as we did not expect to be gone long. For some reason I decided to go back up to the Tower a little while later and was horrified to find that the candle had just flopped over and the whole desk was on fire!

I called for help and ran to get a wet towel from Sean's bathroom. I threw the towel over everything and we managed put the fire out. I got some of Mother's writing wet, but we saved the Tower.

Mark came and told us that the force was very angry. We had just been working on the chapters of *Climb the Highest Mountain* that dealt with black magic and Armageddon. Mother and Mark did a clearance. Mark taught that black magic can cause fires.

Mark said that in this case it was Lucifer himself who had caused the fire, seeking to interfere with the work of the masters. On other occasions it has been members of the Indian Black Brotherhood that have been at work behind fires.

These black magicians from the East have attained the mastery to control elementals and cause them to act against the children of the light. Working with false hierarchs on inner levels, they imprison fiery salamanders by black magic and misuse of the science of mantra. They send them to carry out their curses, causing calamities, accidents and fires.

Fires can have many causes, of course. Sometimes they are accidents or simply caused by human carelessness. Sometimes wildfires are a means directed by God for the elementals to clear records of mankind's discord and purify the earth through the fire element itself. But when there was a fire threatening our community and Mother sensed that it was not the work of God but a manifestation of forces of darkness, she often found that it was the Indian Black Brotherhood that was behind it.

This highlights the importance of our calls for the protection of Archangel Michael when we are on the path. If we seek to advance on the path of chelaship, if we wish to hold a greater light and really make a difference on the planet, the forces of darkness won't be happy about that. We need to seal ourselves and our work in the protection of the angels of the first ray. Mother has said on many occasions that the masters can only give us as much light as we can protect and hold in harmony.

Mark Acts the Fool

Mother said that a lot of people love the ascended master Lanello with a passion but would not have liked Mark Prophet at all if they had met him in person. Actually, Mother said some people could not stand Mark.

At one conference Mark was giving a beautiful esoteric lecture, when suddenly he began to stumble and become almost a bumbling idiot standing there at the podium. After a while a man in the audience got up and left. From my perspective I could not blame him, as Mark's performance deteriorated significantly. After this man left Mark continued giving his beautiful lecture.

It seemed to me that Mark had done this deliberately. When it was all over, at the conclusion of the dictation that followed, I said, "Mark, why in the world did you do that?"

Mark explained, "Well, he wasn't meant to be here for the dictation, so I had to get rid of him some way. Morya did not want him to hear his dictation."

Why would Morya not want this man to hear his dictation? One possible explanation is found in a dictation by El Morya from 1985. The master said:

> Our dictations are not intended for those who are in the world and who have not even approached the

level of being student. The setting forth of the Law and the Light and the release of the dispensations is absolutely essential, and so is the stepping down and the interpretation of that Word by the Holy Spirit through yourselves to those who must have presented to them that which they can take in of this Word.[12]

Another possible reason is that the forcefield where a dictation takes place is hallowed ground and it needs to be protected. The messenger must hold his attunement with the I AM Presence and with the master who is about to speak. This is a delicate process, and so is the delivery of the blessing that the masters release during a dictation. There is a filigree forcefield of light-substance that is formed in the room, which the masters use to release their light.

The presence of people who are not supportive of what is going to take place can be a hindrance to the delivery of a dictation. They can be focuses of darkness or negative energy that would interfere with the receiving of a dictation or the delivery of the light that the master wants to anchor in the world.

On one occasion when Mark was delivering a dictation in a small sanctuary in the city of New York, a lady in the congregation decided she had to get up and leave in the middle of it because she had a bus to catch. This caused such a disruption in the forcefield that the thread of contact with the master was broken and the rest of the dictation was lost.

It is a great blessing to be present for a dictation by one of the ascended masters—and also a great responsibility. Each one present has a responsibility for creating the chalice into which the masters can release their light. We can understand from this story one aspect of the care the masters took in preparing that chalice.

We can also see that Mark was truly a Zen master, like El Morya. He was willing to be a "fool for Christ"—to act the fool and be misunderstood in order to be obedient to his master.

"I Can't" Means "I Won't"

Once I said to Mark, "I can't!" He then told me, "'I can't' means 'I won't.'"

The words "I can't" refer to our ability—or our perception of our ability—to get a job done. While it is important to be practical and to have a realistic assessment of what Saint Germain calls "the realm of the possible," yet often the words "I can't" come from the human mind putting its foot down and refusing to even attempt what needs to be done. "I can't" means I am not willing to even try.

It is always the lesser self that says, "I can't." For isn't it true that God can do anything? And isn't our Higher Self one with God? And isn't everything possible if we are one with God and that Higher Self? So the "I can't" is often the human self refusing to come up higher, not wanting to transcend itself, being unwilling to become one with God, which would make all things possible.

Mother and Mark would often give people very challenging assignments—sometimes things that seemed humanly impossible to accomplish. And indeed they were humanly impossible. That was the whole point. The chela had to surrender his dependence on the outer self and rely on God to accomplish the task.

Some people took these tests as initiations on the path and found through them the means to come up higher and truly transcend themselves. Others, not understanding the nature of the initiation, or perhaps not having the heart of a chela, developed a sense of injustice. They thought it was unfair to be asked to do more than they thought they could.

Another strategy that the messengers employed to help a chela advance on the path was to have that chela change to a new job or a different assignment from the one that the chela might prefer. This was often a direct assignment from a master for the testing of the soul. The chela might need to develop mastery on a different ray, or perhaps a new field of service was necessary in order to balance a particular element of karma.

Annice, as a seasoned chela, rarely if ever refused an assignment from the messengers. She was always willing to take on a new task and to do the best that she could. She knew her limitations but was willing to stretch herself and trust that God would be the doer, even when her human self was not sufficient for the task at hand.

A key element of chelaship as the messengers taught it was to be willing to do whatever was the need of the hour, whatever must be done in order to complete the masters' work —whether it was sorting the mail, cooking a meal for the staff, cleaning the rooms or setting up a bookstore. Whether a task was seemingly important or menial made no difference. One had to be willing to serve according to the need of the hour. This is what it meant to be a member of the staff of the messengers in a time of training, testing and chelaship.

Mark Discovers a Past Life and Is Not Pleased

One day Mark found out from Morya that he had been embodied as the French King Louis XIV.

Mark was aghast. He said to me, "Mrs. Booth, Louis XIV was not a *moral man.*"

Mark accented and drew out the words "moral man," and Annice mimicked him saying it.

I tried to comfort him by saying, "Well, Mark, you are now."

Mark said, "That doesn't make up for it."

That really shook him up.

It is humbling to hear of this episode from the life of our messenger. The Two Witnesses, Mark and Mother, came into embodiment bearing their karma, or as is spoken of in the Bible, "clothed in sackcloth."[13] Any one of us, even a messenger, might have a past life that we are not proud of. This reminds us to not take ourselves or our past lives, good or bad, too seriously. What matters is what we do with the present.

Mother gave an interesting insight into the life of Louis

XIV in a lecture she delivered in 1981. She explained that Louis was subjected to court intrigue projected against him, and also black magic and even Satanism. All of this contributed to him succumbing to the seductions of a number of mistresses—the cause of Mark's remorse.

These kinds of things may have happened to any one of us in a previous life. We may have had good intentions and sought to bring truth and enlightenment to our fellow man, but not had the strength to stand against the forces of darkness that opposed us and our mission. If we would win our ascension in this life, we must overcome that karma, as the messengers have done. And in this day the masters have brought us the spiritual tools we need to defend our mission and our goal of reunion with God.

The shortcomings of Louis XIV are not the whole story of his life. He was known as the Sun King for good reason. He sought to bring in a golden age in France, and the great palace and gardens of Versailles are an outpicturing of his soul memory of the culture and beauty of Venus.

A Meal for Two Queens

At one time there was a young man on the staff who had owned and operated a macrobiotic restaurant before he found the Summit. Mother loved the food that he cooked for her. When he was about to go on vacation, she told him to show me how to cook a particular dish that was a favorite.

When he left I cooked this meal in a skillet—leftover rice and carrots and tahini and soy sauce and other bits and pieces. I was sitting with Mother in the kitchen eating this food and chewing away, when Mother said to me, "You are just the best macrobiotic cook I have ever seen. This is a meal fit for two queens."

Well, the first time Mother said this, I just let it go by—but then she said it again. And finally she said to me, "I will just have to ask Mark who you were."

Right at that moment Mark walked into the kitchen on his way to another part of the house. So Mother asked him, "Mark, who was she? I know that she is a queen sitting at this table."

Mark said, "Oh, she was Vashti." And he walked out the door, just like that, leaving the two of us staring at each other. We had never heard of Vashti. So we looked it up in the Bible.

Vashti was the Queen of King Ahasuerus of Persia, who was Xerxes. She ruled over a huge kingdom and was said to be very beautiful. One day there was an enormous banquet and the men, who were getting drunk, said to the King, "Bring your beautiful wife here that we may look upon her. We want to see how beautiful she is."

Vashti refused to exhibit herself to a group of drunken men and she declined to attend. Apparently there was a minority group of Jewish people in the Kingdom and they used the situation to plot against her. They reminded the king that the punishment for disobeying the order of the King was to be put to death.

This put Xerxes in an awful situation. The king really loved her, but he had to obey his own order or lose face and lose the respect and control of his people. So rather than put her to death he exiled her and put Esther, a Jewish woman, in her place as queen.

Annice told me that Esther later embodied as Annice's sister Mary May. And therein lies the tale of two sisters.

Annice was the oldest of three sisters. The middle one she did not particularly get along with, and the youngest was the reincarnation of Esther. Her little sister looked up to her. Annice thought she was just the cutest thing, and they got along fine.

Mark said that Vashti had resented that Esther had taken over her kingdom, and their karma required that the two be born in the same family to experience the sibling rivalry and enmity between family members, which is a frequent sign of karma and karmic entanglements. However, relationships within a family also provide the opportunity to balance much karma through love and service to one another. Mark was pleased to hear that Annice got on so well with her younger sister and said that this was a sign that she had transmuted her karma from the life of Vashti and Esther.

The life as Vashti was not the only life where Annice was embodied as a queen. In later years a Keeper of the Flame phoned Annice and said, "You probably don't remember me, but I used to know you. Can you settle an argument for me? Were you Mary, Queen of Scots, and Queen Victoria?"

Annice was astounded at the rumors that go around in our small community and amazed at the boldness of this person in asking such a question. Nevertheless, she answered, "The messengers confirmed that I was Mary, Queen of Scots. As to Queen Victoria, I do not know. The messengers did not tell me that."

No one seems to know where the idea began that Annice had been embodied as Queen Victoria. It didn't originate with Annice herself, and it doesn't seem to be something that Mark or Mother ever said.

A few years earlier, when Annice was traveling to Europe with the messengers, they were out on the deck of the *SS Bremen*. Mark and Mother looked at each other and said, "Oh, I know who she was!" But then they said, "Morya says that we can't tell you." So Annice probably never did find out what that lifetime was.

Once a Cardinal

Mark was speaking to a staff member one day when I walked in the room. Mark said, "Ohhh. Do you see what I see? She was Cardinal Mazarin."

It was in this informal way that Mark told me who I was in the time of Louis XIV. This Cardinal raised young Louis until the age of fourteen and taught him how to rule.

I was very fortunate to have Mark to explain things to me. Mark usually told me everything that he had to say to me in front of others, often in front of everyone. I learned to not be attached, because I never knew if it was going to be good or bad.

At times there is a thinning of the veil and our past lives come to the fore. And it must have been the time for Annice to know about this former life.

It was a blessing for Annice that she knew Mark. He had the ability to see beyond the veil. On this occasion, when God showed him one of Annice's past lives, he shared it with her and with another chela, who also had this inner sight.

One might think it would be interesting or perhaps even helpful to know who one was in a past life. However, it can be a mixed blessing. Once we know of a past life, the karma of that life is opened and we have to deal with it. If we are ready, there is the opportunity to transmute that karma and to more consciously integrate the lessons learned and the positive momentums of that life. If we are not ready, the burden of records and karma may be a hindrance to our service in this life.

This is one reason why it is best not to probe into our past. There is a reason for the veil of forgetfulness that seals us from the records of many lifetimes. The masters will show us what we need to know when we are ready and when it will be helpful to our path. But they keep many things sealed from us when we are not ready to deal with them.

Annice did not take pride in her past lives. She knew that it does not matter who we were—we have all had famous and not so famous lives. The lesson is nonattachment. What is important is to balance our karma and do the best in this life to win our immortal reunion with God.

An Old Sailor

On one occasion Peter and I were burdened when a former member of our organization sent an email worldwide criticizing us. Amongst other things, this person claimed that Peter and I had been embodied as the Roman Emperor Justinian and his wife Theodora. The messengers have spoken of these two as fallen ones who had perverted the true teachings of Christ and remade the Christian church to serve their political ambitions.

The individual who wrote the letter was claiming to be a messenger and also claiming to be the incarnation of Serapis Bey, so we didn't take his accusation too seriously. But the letter was full of anger and venom, and we were feeling burdened by the energy and weight of darkness of the false hierarchy that was working through this individual. The criticism hung like a heavy weight over us, removing any sense of joy in life.

Annice told me to "reverse the tide" of this energy—to not accept the curses and black magic that were contained in the letter, to not accept the negative energy, and to call for it to be returned to the one who sent it forth. We did this, but we were still burdened. The energy made it hard to think, to function well, or even to do our work.

At a publications meeting with Peter and myself, Annice sensed the energy we were feeling. She then told me to take out my notebook, and she spoke to us both:

The fact that he called you Justinian and Theodora is neither here nor there. Even if you were, you are not that person now. You are Rev. Peter Duffy and Rev. Neroli Duffy, ministers of the church.

Let me tell you what Mark once told me about one of my past lives. He never took me aside to tell me these things by myself. This was in front of a room full of staff.

Suddenly Mark said to me, "Oh, my God! Mrs. Booth, I can see that you were an old sailor. You were almost ready for your ascension and you made so much karma in that embodiment that we were all relieved that you were not going to be taken away from us.

"Whatever bad deeds you associate with a sailor, you did them all. You had the foulest mouth, the handiest fists, you had a woman in every port. All you identify with a sailor in the worst way—that was you in that lifetime!"

Annice laughed remembering the incident.

I was mortified, but I had the presence of mind to say, "Thank you, Mark."

Annice went on to tell us how to handle the situation we were facing.

Instead of being bowed down by the energy, keep moving! You don't know if you were. You probably were not. But even if you were, you are not that person now. These are projections. Roll them back. The statements that were written are nothing but a curse. No matter what, it is just a bunch of nonsense.

Mark used to say occasionally to me, "Remember that old sailor." It kept me humble. It reminded me that we are who we are, in spite of what we think we are. We are not our past lives. We are immortal, God-free beings. We are the same soul wearing different sets of clothing throughout the centuries.

If we had all had only holy embodiments we would be ascended and not here at all. The fallen angels try to get you pegged. Instead, you must say, "What is that to thee? Follow thou me!" Say it a thousand million times if necessary.

One never knows what one has done in a past life—good or ill. Only a messenger can know for sure, and at the time we were dealing with these accusations, our messenger was retired and we were not able to ask her. And even if we had asked her, she may well have simply said exactly what Annice told us. Because in the end, it doesn't matter who we were or what we might have done in a past life. What matters is what we make of the opportunities of this life.

We later found out that we were not embodied as Justinian and Theodora. The messenger has said that Theodora passed through the halls of The Summit Lighthouse many years ago and left. Although these embodiments were not ours, it was an important lesson about not being attached to one's past lives, either good or bad—ours or anyone else's. Many people who had past lives they would rather have not known about went on to make their ascension, including Mark.

Annice was frank in discussing her past life with us and I appreciated her example. Did my knowledge of Annice's past life as a sailor change my attitude towards her? Not at all. The ascended masters do not care who we have been in the past—they care about what we are doing with the present. This understanding helps us to be less attached to the good or the bad about ourselves, even as we strive to do the best that we can and balance the karma of all of our past lives.

Someone seeing the record of this past life of Annice might think she couldn't be a very holy person. But there is an old saying that sometimes the greatest sinners make the greatest saints. The Bible says that it is better to be hot or cold, for if we are lukewarm, God says, "I will spue thee out of my mouth." The one with the most karma or the most difficult past may be sincerely penitent and move swiftly to make up the difference. Saint Francis lived a riotous life until his conversion. Judas Iscariot had great remorse for his role in the betrayal and crucifixion of Jesus and made his ascension at the end of his next life.

"What is that to thee? Follow thou me!" were the words of Jesus to the apostle James. It is a simple but profound message. There are all sorts of things we could worry about—what people say or think about us, what we might have done or not done. But we can't let any of these things divert our attention from the path.

No Bad Karma Together

One time Mark and I were just chitchatting. Mark looked at me and said, "Mrs. Booth, I don't think that you and I have any bad karma."

I said to him, "That's nice."

You never could tell what was going through Mark's mind.

It was fortunate that Annice did not have bad karma with Mark. However it was not the same for some other staff members, who had personal karma with Mark or Mother. Part of their experience with the messengers was for the balancing of that karma, and many came through the doors of The Summit Lighthouse for that very purpose.

Family Ties

In these days, especially since the advent of email, problems in our organization often come from within—from our own staff and members who are disgruntled or from former members. The force uses division to project inharmony and disunity as well as dissatisfaction itself, and this in turn breeds more division.

It was different in the years that Mark was with us. There was great harmony then within the small staff, but there were inevitably problems that came from the outside. Mark was sometimes greatly burdened by projections or intrusions of negative energy.

One source of this opposition was psychic groups who copied our *Pearls of Wisdom* and dictations. For example the group called Mark Age sent out letters, and there was a group called Ruby Ray Focus at Sedona, Arizona, that caused problems for Mark. In those days, we did not have a decree tag* to support Mark as we did later for Mother. However, Mark had

---

* A tag was a pool of permanent staff members who volunteered to decree for Mother to provide spiritual defense against opposition to the mission. It was called a *tag* because you stayed at your post (usually one to three hours) until the next person came to relieve you. Usually a tag consisted of two or three people decreeing together at Mother's house or wherever she was working at the time. These sessions were often challenging. But you got a real sense of the effort and sheer determination needed to deal with the opposition to the work of the Brotherhood on earth.

Mother supporting him and he had the wholehearted support of his staff.

Many of the problems of opposition showed up as illness in Mark's physical body. In the early days of the Summit, Mark had a bleeding stomach ulcer. One day as he took a dictation from the Ascended Lady Master Nada, he could taste the blood as it gurgled up from his stomach into his throat. During the dictation Nada healed him and the symptoms were alleviated immediately. At other times he was plagued by prostate problems.

At one time I was helping Mother with *Climb the Highest Mountain* at La Tourelle and I was also House Mother at the Motherhouse in Santa Barbara. On one of my trips to Santa Barbara, I visited my younger sister. She was very interested in the Summit and yet equally interested in anything that was psychic. (She has since had a heart attack and died—like all of the other members of my family.) She had found some group who told her that by sticking pins into a doll in a certain place in the anatomy of the doll, you could affect a person.

I asked her, "What place do you mean?"

She said, "The prostate, of course."

I understood immediately that she was sticking pins into a doll that represented Mark Prophet and that this was contributing to his prostate problem. I was mortified. How could my sister do such a thing? I quickly told Mark what my sister was doing.

When I returned to Colorado Springs, Mark met me at the airport. I said to him, "Mark, I certainly hope that I can make up to you in service the damage my sister is doing to you." It was one of those times that he looked right through me and did not say a word.

At this point in the conversation, Annice turned to me and said, "You are very fortunate with your family." My family fully supports my being a student of the ascended masters, and my mother is also a member of the organization. Annice continued:

Later that evening Mark and Mother called me into the prayer room in the Tower and told me that they had done a clearance on me. I was very fortunate to have had personal interaction with them. Mark told me that the Lords of Karma had said they were cutting me completely free from all of my relatives. The only catch was that my sympathy could reactivate those ties, and if I allowed that to happen I would lose the dispensation.

I was amazed. I have never felt such a complete clearance. I would think of one of my family members and there was no more energy associated with them than if I had been reading a name in a telephone book.

I have been vigilant ever since to be careful about human sympathy. If I would get a letter or a communication from a family member or if they were thinking about me, sending energy to me, I would immediately cancel out any feelings that were not at the level of the Christ. I would be careful not to indulge in any feeling of "poor so and so" or "what a shame." I would love my family and have compassion for their plight, but I would not engage their human consciousness or human nonsense. I would love them from the level of the Christ.

This was quite a lesson for Annice—and for all of us—in the nature of family relationships. Annice was horrified and also mystified as to why her sister would intentionally try to harm others through black magic. She wondered how on earth she ended up in the same family with such a person.

One answer, of course, is karma.

Before we take embodiment we are assigned the family we will be born into. We have often known our family members from past lives with them. The relationships may be the same or different. We can be a daughter in one life and then mother to the same soul in the next.

We may be placed with particular souls because of good karma together from the past so we can support one another in our missions. For example, Mary had been Jesus' mother in a previous life and was therefore well prepared to support him in his mission in that final embodiment.

We may also be assigned to particular souls because of negative karma from the past. If this is the case, we are required to love and serve one another until our karma is balanced and we are free to move on.

Mother demonstrated the overcoming of very difficult karmic circumstances in her own family. Some of this she describes in the book of her memoirs, *In My Own Words*. We are told that these intense karmic ties are common in an individual's final embodiment, when the soul seeks to do the utmost to balance all of her karma before the ascension.

Karma also explains why family members may be very different from one another. For example, through interactions over the centuries, many lightbearers have made karma with very dark souls when these fallen ones subjected them to anger or persecution and they responded in kind. The skeins of karma have therefore tied the lightbearers to the fallen ones and they are required to interact with them very personally in a family situation. The natural love that exists between family members and the many opportunities for mutual service provide a means to balance that karma. Therefore you can never judge a family by its individual members: in any given family you may have side by side the seed of light and the embodied seed of the wicked.

However, difficult family relationships are not always due to karma. Some chelas have been told by the messenger that they deliberately chose to come into a family with individuals of great darkness. There may have been a lesson they needed to learn from this personal interaction with evil. A lightbearer might also be placed in a particular family so that the dark ones in that family would constantly have an example and a reminder of a higher way. This is an opportunity for them to turn around, serve the light, and make their own way back to God. But if they reject this opportunity, if instead they turn against that lightbearer in their midst and persecute that one, then the child of light may also become the instrument of the judgment of parents and family members who are not of the light.

Sometimes the only reason that lightbearers have been born into families of fallen ones is so that they could reclaim their genes. Long ago the fallen ones stole the genes of the sons and daughters of God. And often the only way to reclaim that genetic inheritance is to be born physically through those particular people and their ancestral lineage.

In assigning souls to families the Karmic Board has a difficult task, but they make the best possible decisions for the benefit and greatest opportunity for all souls.

This incident that Annice describes conveys an understanding of family relationships from the ascended masters' perspective, which is one that Jesus also taught. The story is told in the Bible of a disciple approaching the master as he was teaching, telling him that his mother and his brethren were waiting. Jesus replied, "Whosoever shall do the will of God, the same is my brother, and my sister, and my mother."[14]

Jesus is teaching us that the flesh-and-blood relationships of human families are not the most important ones in the life of a disciple. He was showing the impersonal nature of the Christ, which relates to all on the basis of spiritual values rather than family ties. All who do the will of the Father are a part of the true family of God.

Another teaching Jesus gave on families is that "a man's foes shall be they of his own household."[15] It may be that we have those who are aligned with darkness in our families. But it may also be that family members are not of themselves evil people, but may unwittingly become the instruments of forces of darkness seeking to deter us from our homeward journey— as the fallen ones always seek the weakest link, the point of vulnerability, by which to attack the lightbearer. When we understand this, we learn not to take these things personally and we remember to make calls for the protection of loved ones and family members.

The ascended masters teach that it is lawful to love and care for family members, but we should not allow them to stand in the way of our own pursuit of the spiritual path or our mission in this life. The messengers have taught their staff and students to maintain their family ties, but to do so at the level of the Christ consciousness. This means that we relate to family members from the level of the heart and with true love and compassion, not allowing ourselves to be drawn into ties at the level of the emotional body, including human sympathy, sentimentality or nostalgia.

These ties at the level of human emotions have been described as "family mesmerism." This is a type of energy whereby individuals can hold an inordinate sway over other family members, seeking to control them or cause them to behave in ways that can be detrimental to the soul. This form of emotional or mental abuse can be subtle, but frequently even more damaging to the sensitive soul than physical abuse. Even if one is fortunate to be a part of a loving, happy family, we can all take on the ways and the human consciousness of family members.

The invocations of the messengers could be of tremendous assistance in cutting individuals free from family mesmerism and many other types of negative energies that burden the soul. On a few occasions Mother explained the origins of that which was cleared from students who sought her counsel. However, she rarely gave detailed reports on the clearance work that was done. Once these elements of the human consciousness have been cleared, there is often no purpose in re-examining them in detail. In fact, this can become a form of a psychic hook, luring us to hold on to or even recreate that which has been taken.

The messengers are no longer doing this work on the outer, but we can do our own self-clearance work, especially through the use of dynamic decrees and in group decree sessions. Mother has recommended that we give decrees to Astrea, the Elohim of the fourth ray, to Archangel Michael and the violet flame for our personal clearance work. We can also ask the messengers to make specific calls for us on inner levels. The angels will remove that which they can take according to the Great Law, and it is passed through the flame. This is a process that can be cumulative over a number

Annice, her son, Larry, and her great-grandson. Relationships with family members are often carried over from previous lifetimes, but Annice and Larry were in the unusual situation of having no karma between them from past lives—either good or bad.

of years, as elements of negativity are removed layer by layer, like peeling an onion.

Most importantly, we need to let go of patterns of negativity, including family mesmerism. The angels respect our free will and will not remove that which we are not willing to release. We also need to be vigilant not to recreate what has been taken from us in these clearances. The messengers, the masters and the angels work very hard to secure our freedom from these conditions, and we need to honor their gift and not allow it to be lost.

Don't Personalize Your Work

Annice was reviewing chapter 7 of *Climb the Highest Mountain* when the book was due to be reprinted with a new title, *The Path of the Higher Self*. While reading it, she came across the story of Hypatia, a Greek philosopher, scientist and teacher who lived Egypt in the fourth century AD. This was one of Mother's past embodiments, and in that lifetime she had been murdered by a mob of fanatical Christians.

Annice recalled the time when she had been working on this chapter for the first printing of the book.

I had been working with another staff member on the original volume of *Climb the Highest Mountain* in a tiny, tiny office outside Mother's bedroom. It was a five by six foot linen closet. We managed to fit two chairs and a card table in there.

About 10 or 11 o'clock one night we were working on the chapter that mentioned Hypatia, and the akashic record of her murder must have surfaced.

I turned to my co-worker and said, "Oh my God, I killed her. I killed Hypatia!"

She was feeling the same thing, and she said, "Oh no you didn't. I killed her."

We were both crying and went to Mother and repeated

our stories, each claiming the incident as our own.

Mother said to us, "Now listen here. Both of you go to the sanctuary and do Astreas until you get a hold of yourselves. Come back when you are in a better vibration."

When we returned she said, "I want you to know that working on *Climb the Highest Mountain* is a very high initiation—it is the highest initiation on this staff. You can have all sorts of problems if you personalize this work. Unless you have an impersonal and detached feeling, I cannot work with you."

Mother repeated the lesson that if you feel emotional about a past-life record, if you can still feel the emotion and identify with the record, you have not yet transmuted it.

She later told me that neither of us had been the culprit. The person who killed Hypatia had actually embodied as the mother of a woman we knew. The mother had been a vicious type of person in this life, too.

While working on the section of *Climb the Highest Mountain* that spoke about the martyrdom of Hypatia, Annice and her co-worker had tuned in to the record of the event in akasha. Feeling the intensity of it, they had over-identified with it.

This experience illustrates one danger of probing past lives: it is easy to reach an incorrect conclusion about who we might have been. If we do, we can inadvertently take on a karmic burden or a sense of guilt about something we might not even have done. We might feel something with great intensity, but it is important to remember that one's feelings may not always be a reliable guide. It is only the voice of our Christ Self that can guide us unerringly.

On a number of occasions the messengers came across someone who was burdened about some past life that a psychic had revealed. When they examined the record, they found out that the person had never been who they thought they were.

We also see in this story an example of compassion, as Mother had the opportunity to meet the person who had killed Hypatia. She had to deal with all kinds of people over the years, even those who had killed her in previous lives. She said that she would see these people in the lines of those who came before her for healing calls or blessings. She said that she felt no bitterness or resentment for these people, but only joy to see them come to the place where they could overcome the record and make progress on the spiritual path.

Working on *Climb the Highest Mountain* with Florence Miller

When Mother was working on *Climb the Highest Mountain,* Florence Miller and I were assigned to type her edits. We started at 10 P.M., when the typewriter became available, and worked to 2 A.M.

This was the time before computers, so each time we typed a page we did five carbon copies. If we made a mistake on a page, we would have to retype and reproof that whole page. Even if there was just one mistake, we had to do the page over again. This went on night after night. We often had to redo one single page over and over.

Florence and I estimated that in the course of completing the book we typed each page at least twelve times. Each time we typed it, that teaching was anchored in our four lower bodies.

How fortunate we are now to have computers to save time and labor. This technology would have made the work so much easier for Annice and Florence. But the task had to be accomplished with the tools at hand, so these two souls stayed and stayed and did what had to be done.

Annice and Florence also understood the element of chelaship in their work. The spiritual path requires endurance and the painstaking correction of one's faults. They saw each error they made as representing a mistake in their own consciousness. By retyping the page, they were correcting those errors in consciousness and working through their karma with the masters, with the messengers and with one another.

This reminds us of the story of Milarepa, who as part of his chelaship had to build a house, tear it down and rebuild it many times. This was the means the Guru Marpa used to help him balance his karma, tear down the negative elements of his consciousness, and rebuild on a true foundation. Sometimes the inner work of the soul must have a counterpart in the physical.

By typing and retyping each page, Annice and Florence also came to know the teaching of *Climb the Highest Mountain* very well. Even if they had read the book a number of times, it would not have penetrated as deeply into their consciousness as it did by their typing the words over and over again. One can imagine that this process would have allowed the alchemy of this teaching to enter into other dimensions and compartments of being. In later years Annice taught from this book in her classes at Summit University. She knew exactly what was in each chapter and could often quote the words, even as she had been able to quote the Bible as a young girl.

In addition to the practicalities of publishing a book, the messenger and the masters were providing an avenue for their teaching to be thoroughly grounded in two humble chelas as they worked away into the night. If Annice or Florence had complained or given up, if they had said, "I can't" or "I won't," imagine what they would have missed.

At La Tourelle during a certain period of time Florence was working around the clock, day and night. I said to her, "How do you do it?" Florence said in a small voice, "Coffeeee." Florence drank about thirteen cups of coffee per day.

Florence Miller made her ascension after she passed on in 1979. She had been embodied as the great mystic Saint Teresa of Avila, and we know her today as Ascended Lady Master Kristine.

Sanat Kumara spoke of her example of chelaship in his *Pearls of Wisdom* on "The Opening of the Seventh Seal." He described her as our "co-worker and friend, a chela of El Morya whom I now defend as the example and forerunner on the Path of the Ruby Ray." Florence was absolutely dedicated to the messengers and their mission, and like Annice, served on the Board of Directors of the organization. She worked very long hours when it was needed for a project to be completed. And evidently coffee helped her to get through some of these challenging times.

Annice told me this story not only as an example of dedication on the path, but also to let me know that one cannot push one's body with impunity. Mother once explained to a Summit University class that Florence died too soon because she didn't take care of her health. The masters have told us to be kind to our bodies, since we need to live long enough to balance as much karma as we can so that we can make our ascension.

We can all seek to emulate Florence's dedication to service. But Florence, now the Ascended Lady Master Kristine, might not want us to emulate her coffee consumption. Annice never

151

drank coffee, but she took plenty of water, liked to have tea each day, and drank a Diet Coke from time to time if she needed a boost.

Some people might observe the habits of these two chelas and decide that if they did these things, they must not have much mastery. But they each in their own way did what they needed to do to get a job done for the masters. It is not in outer perfection that the quality of heart of the chela is seen.

Not the Holy Spirit,
But an Angry Wind

I took Annice to breakfast in June 2003, not long before our large annual conference in July. There was some of the usual pre-class opposition, and this day there was a strong wind blowing and raising up the dust everywhere around the conference site. Annice commented on the wind being "angry" and told the following story.

Mother and I were working on the "black" chapters of *Climb the Highest Mountain* [the chapters that dealt with black magic, witchcraft, antichrist and similar subjects]. **There was a huge wind that suddenly blew up outside the window of Mother's third floor bedroom where we were working. It blew the big oak tree that was outside and which was taller than the house. It seemed as if the oak tree was bending over. Mother turned to me and innocently said, "Dear, do you think that this is the wind of the Holy Spirit?"**

I said, "That doesn't sound like any Holy Spirit wind that I have ever heard."

The messengers taught their staff to be aware of energy. When working on a project, you had to have a sense of the opposition to that project and whether the necessary spiritual work was being done to handle it. Any project for the Brotherhood is opposed in some form or another by the forces of darkness, and dealing with those forces is vital if the project is to be completed successfully. The more important the project, the more intense the opposition.

For example, the "black" chapters of *Climb the Highest Mountain* expose the fallen angels and their strategies. These fallen angels do not want to be exposed in this way, so they work on inner levels to prevent this information from being published. An essential part of the work on these chapters was to deal with the forces of darkness that directly opposed that project.

How do you tell if the necessary spiritual work is being done? Sensitivity to energy and an awareness of what is happening around you will often give the clues that you need.

How are you feeling?

Is there a sense of weight or oppression?

Are you feeling out of sorts?

Are you having difficulty thinking or focusing on the task?

Are there many interruptions and miscommunications?

Are other people bowed down by opposition?

Are there accidents or unexpected delays?

Are things just not happening as they should?

Any of these things might be a sign of opposition to a project.

Be aware of the elementals also, since they often reflect and outpicture the energies of other planes, in this case in an angry wind.

The bottom line is that if something does not feel right, it may well be an indication that you need to get to work spiritually and roll back the energy. It is not a matter of being superstitious or psychic, but of having a realistic assessment of the forces of light and darkness in your world.

Be aware of energy and what you need to do to deal with it in order to complete a project. Sometimes you need to stop and make some calls or do some decrees in order to make progress. Sometimes you just need to press on against all odds and get the job done.

"You Are a Son of God"

Mother gave a side comment to me while we were working on *Climb the Highest Mountain*. We came to a paragraph about the sons and daughters of God and the children of God, and I commented that I really did not know which one I was—a son of God or a child of God.

Mother said, "My goodness, Annice. You are a son of God. You have had many more initiations than the children of God. You are one of the ones who came with Sanat Kumara from Venus with me and Mark.* You previously came with us and Morya from Mercury."

The children of God are newer souls. They need direction and shepherding and the compassion of the teachings. They cannot stand the full thrust of the law. They need direction from the sons and daughters of God who are meant to be the teachers of the children of God.

Annice had quite a degree of humility, and it shows in this story. She didn't see herself as anyone important, and she was humble enough to ask the question, not assuming that she had

---

* The moving story of Sanat Kumara and of those who came with him to planet earth on the rescue mission (the first Keepers of the Flame) can be found in Elizabeth Clare Prophet, *The Opening of the Seventh Seal: Sanat Kumara on the Path of the Ruby Ray* (Gardiner, Mont.: The Summit Lighthouse Library, 2001), pp. 10–15.

a higher calling. Mother apparently thought it was important for her to know something of her spiritual heritage.

When I think of humility, I often recall the prayer in the *Sacred Ritual for Keepers of the Flame*, "Keep me humble before Thee, positive to the world." There is a false humility that appears to be humble but in fact is quite proud, wanting to be thought well of by others for appearing humble. There is also a false humility that is an accepting of the condemnation of the fallen ones, that would seek to prevent a son or daughter of God from ever rising up to fulfill a mission or a calling to leadership. The sense of being positive to the world is quite compatible with the true inner humility that is the undergarment of the saints.

Annice indeed fulfilled the calling of a son of God. She shepherded many sons and daughters of God as well as children of God. Under the messenger's guidance she gave them direction and taught them to teach others about the spiritual path.

The Soul Always Knows

In the Holy Land tour in 1972, when we were at Baalbek, the vibrations were very bad as we walked through the ruins of the old temples. Mark told me, "I do not want my children to step in these rooms at all. I'll hold this child and you hold the other two." I held the two girls, Erin and Moira, and Mark had Sean.

Mark told me that these were the cubicles where the priests took the temple virgins and raped them before they killed them. We walked to a precipice that dropped into a deep chasm and a pool. Mark said, "That's where they threw them over."

I said to him, "Mark, this is awful. I can tell that I have been here before, but I do not know if I was a priest or a victim."

I went on to ask him a question. "Mark, what I want to know is this. Say I had been a priest and I was faithfully following my religion, being faithful to Baal, who I thought mistakenly was my Lord. What kind of karma would I make if I was just following orders?"

Mark looked at me very seriously and said, "Mrs. Booth the soul knows. Even if you think that you are following your god, the soul knows right from wrong and you are still accountable." He would not tell me which I had been. But I suspect that I had been a priest.

This was a very important lesson. We have all followed our gods and thought that we were right. Perhaps there were many sincere devotees of Baal. That was the culture of the time and the gods that we followed. We were lightbearers in a dark culture.

Therefore look neither to the right nor the left. Let God be true and every man a liar.

There is a certain amount of grace that is allowed us so that first we can come close to the messengers and become aware of the masters. It is a grace that we have the mantle and the acuity to be able to understand these teachings and compile these books.

Annice then said to me:

Look at the books you are writing. You had the training to be a doctor, a minister, a teaching assistant at Summit University, to work for the messenger and for me. You compiled the book *Wanting to Be Born*.

Annice was referring to a book I had recently written giving the ascended masters' perspective on abortion. I told Annice that I had wondered why I was the one to write this book. I had never been pregnant in this life, had always been against abortion and had never had an abortion or encouraged others to have abortions. Annice said:

In ancient Rome abortion was a common form of contraception. We probably all had them back then. All of this certainly keeps us humble. We never know what we might have done or not done, so we cannot be proud.

We do not know our own karma, and each one is unique. Look at my own son. Mother said to me, "I have looked and looked in akasha and I cannot find a single soul with whom you have a karma that required you to bring them into embodiment. That is so unusual. Usually you see a mother and a whole string of souls that she could bring into embodiment."

We cannot judge by this life. We have all been on the wrong side at some time or another. We need to have compassion for one another and for ourselves and not be quick to judge.

It is unfortunate that people tend to want to peg others the way they knew them a year ago or ten years ago. In spiritual terms it is called "holding a matrix" about someone. Holding a negative mental image of another can really hamper their progress spiritually and at all levels.

Mother was the champion of the soul of all of her staff and all of her students. She encouraged them to hold the highest vision for one another, as she did. She was the shepherd of souls and was aware of their progress. Mother explained that Mark Prophet built an organization because he truly understood that people are changing every minute. You have to give them opportunity, for they do change.

The Rice Fast

Mark Prophet was always interested in health foods and fasting. On one occasion he started a ten-day rice fast, and Annice did it with him. On the eighth day, Mark decided he should end his fast. Annice was feeling fine, and Mark said she could continue as long as she stayed close to him so he could watch her aura.

At lunch time, Mark noticed something wasn't quite right with Annice. What had happened was that she had fasted so long she was no longer fully tethered to her body. She felt wonderful. She was in a kind of blissful reverie and her consciousness was somewhere off in the etheric. She did not recall doing any work that day, just floating up and down the stairs.

On the last day of that rice fast, all I had done was walk up and down the stairs all day.

Mark thundered at me, "You are through with fasting!"

I said, "Mark! Why are you mad at me? I did exactly as you asked."

Mark said, "I'm mad at you because Morya's mad at me! I let you get out of your body. Before you took embodiment you promised to stay in your body and work!"

It is apparently very easy for me to leave my body and

float off to higher realms. So in this life, I do not fast and I don't see things or have high spiritual experiences. This is a lifetime to work.

We do have different lives for different purposes, and we can express different aspects of our Causal Bodies in different lives. In a similar way, we might work on a different chakra each lifetime.

Annice has a reputation of being very down-to-earth and concrete. And yet she could detect the radiation of light very quickly and a wrong vibration even more quickly. Once you knew her you gained the impression that she could have very high spiritual experiences if she were to try to do so by fasting, extended meditation or other means. In fact, you suspect that she would not spend very much time in her body at all if she pursued that path—but that was not her assignment in this life.

Although fasting is a means to cleanse the four lower bodies, remove toxins and impurities and balance karma, we need to be careful in our practice of fasting. The masters do not recommend that their disciples undertake fasts lasting longer than three days unless they are directly under the guidance and protection of a master or a messenger, as Annice was in this case.

There are potential dangers in prolonged fasting, not only physical but spiritual. If the soul is not fully anchored in the body or if the aura is weakened through excessive fasting, there is the potential for demon possession. Annice's experience shows the importance of having spiritual sponsorship for a long fast. Mark was able to intercede when Annice was having a problem and was not even aware of it herself.

Mark's Mastery of Meditation

Morya once said that Mark could go in and out of meditation as fast as he had ever seen anyone go—it was just like an elevator.

For most of us, it's not that easy to meditate or raise our consciousness to a higher plane. In contrast, it's not difficult to lower our consciousness. Sometimes all it takes is to watch television for a while or mingle with a crowd at the mall.

Of course, it is necessary to focus our attention firmly in the physical octave when we have work to do there and karma to balance. However, we often don't find it easy to raise our consciousness to higher planes again after being focused in these realms. After a day on the job, it takes time and energy to make our spiritual attunement. Some people find that music can help. Decrees can also be very effective.

Mark could do it almost instantly, simply by an act of will. This was one of the qualities that enabled him to be such a fine instrument for the masters.

More Memories of Mark

A few years after Mother's retirement, Annice planned a weekend with Mark Prophet for the anniversary of his ascension. She had awoken early one morning, and still in her nightgown, she sat at her desk and wrote down the outline. She felt that Mark had given it to her. I could well believe this, as I felt the Holy Spirit when she spoke of her plans.

She did not know that the managers of the organization were also meeting and sharing their own ideas for this event. But it was Annice's plan that was adopted, and she made it clear that she was the one with the matrix. It was her idea and she would decide on the details.

She spoke of the times with Mother in the days after Mark's ascension. It was like the forty days after Jesus' resurrection, when the disciples were all gathered in the Upper Room receiving the most precious teachings from the master. For forty days the staff were in the upper room in the Causal Body of Lanello.

She also shared a few other memories of Mark Prophet.

Mark was a devotee of Mother Mary. He simply stated that he would not have made it without her.

* * *

One day Mark was so burdened by the energy that he couldn't take it any more. He stood in front of the huge picture of Morya in the library to talk to the master, but he was so distressed that he started to give the call numbers of his radio!

* * *

After Mark's heart attack, there was a huge roar that could be heard all throughout La Tourelle.

I said, "My stars! What was that?"

I went to talk to Mark. Apparently Morya had told him, "Well, are you just going to lay there and be sick, or are you going to roar like the lion that you are?"

So he did. Mark roared like a lion and the sound could be heard all over La Tourelle.

The lion is the symbol of St. Mark, his embodiment as the scribe.

* * *

A long-time member of the Summit, Isabelle Dirkers, had gone to grammar school with Mark, and she told us where his house was back then. Chippewa Falls was across the Mississippi from Minneapolis. One time David Drye and I took a trip out there to see the house.

Some other people found out about it later, and when they were postering there for a lecture in North Minneapolis, they stopped to see Mark's house, talked to the woman who owned it and asked to see her attic. They told her that they knew someone who had lived there and who had prayed in the attic.

I thought that this showed poor taste and attunement, and I wish that they had not done it. The owner kicked them out and the house was off-limits to anyone from The Summit Lighthouse from that time on.

Small Unexpected Statements

We were finalizing the first volume of *Climb the Highest Mountain* and everyone was supposed to do nothing but work on the book. We were not even supposed to stop for decrees.

I was wearing polyester dresses at the time and I found that they were all dirty. I took them to wash them in the laundry room. Mark came to the laundry room and said, "What are you doing here Mrs. Booth? You are supposed to be working on the book."

I became flip and I said, "I agree that this is a waste of time. I think that the violet flame should wash the clothes, don't you?"

Mark got very serious and looked straight through me and said, "Yes, Mrs. Booth. You are absolutely right. You get just that close to God and the violet flame will do your laundry for you."

Then he simply turned on his heel and walked away. No one could look through you like Mark could, and no one who wasn't there knows what it was really like to live with that man.

Many of the most important lessons that I learned from Mark Prophet came in small sentences like this at unexpected times.

Have you ever noticed how God has ways of letting you know when you are not where you need to be in vibration or consciousness? It was probably no accident that the messenger came into the laundry room at that exact moment.

On the outer, Annice was still quite new to the path—she had first met Mark Prophet less than six years earlier. The Annice of later years would not have spoken this way. But in this case she was flippant. She knew after she had spoken that her response was not an adequate one. Instead of admitting she was not where she needed to be and accepting that she had been caught, she answered back.

Mark's response was very interesting. He did not react to what he might have seen as a lack of respect for him or even the masters' teachings. Instead, he gave her a higher vision of the spiritual path.

One of the reasons God sends messengers is that our human consciousness tends to react badly when we are challenged or corrected. If we react in this way towards a messenger (a human being who may have faults), the karma is not as severe as it would be if we reacted badly to one of the ascended masters. Thus the masters often remain "behind the veil" while we work out our negative momentums.

Mother has said that she wears the mantle of messenger twenty-four hours a day. In airports, restaurants or in the most humble or unlikely places, the master could speak through her. An important part of the path of chelaship was to learn to receive what might come through the messenger with grace and good cheer.

More Lessons from Past Lives

Another unexpected situation happened with Mother at this same time, when we were finishing our work on *Climb the Highest Mountain*. One Sunday Mother turned to me and said, "Annice, I think you should go to a movie." It was the biggest shock that I could imagine at a time when we were working so hard to finish the book and get it to the printers.

I said, "A movie?"

"Yes, a movie."

"Which one?"

"Look in the newspaper and you'll know which one."

Mary, Queen of Scots was showing at the local movie theater. The film was about Mary and her conflict with Elizabeth I of England. Elizabeth was responsible for having Mary beheaded.

I said, "Well, I've always been fascinated by that period of history, and I could never understand which of those two women was right." So I took a bus to the movie and I watched it. When I returned Mother said, "What did you learn?"

By that time I had figured out that Mary, Queen of Scots, was one of my embodiments. I said to her, "Well, I knew that I was Queen of Scotland but I did not realize that I was also Queen of France."

It was my use of the word "I" which caused Mother to react immediately. She said to me, "Now you listen here. You go right into the chapel and decree. Whenever you can still identify with the lifetime, you have not transmuted it. Go do Astreas until it has become an impersonal part of your life."

Throughout the years, Annice was shown some of her past lives by the messengers. Sometimes the masters will reveal a life to us through a movie or a book or some other means which will clue us into that life. They show them to us when we are ready.

It is interesting to note that the soul of Elizabeth I had been embodied earlier as Joan of Arc and later as Benjamin Franklin and Edna Ballard, Saint Germain's messenger from the 1930s until 1972. As a messenger, she wrote under the pen name Lotus Ray King, and we know her today as the Ascended Lady Master Lotus. Her twin flame is the Ascended Master Godfre, who had embodied as Richard the Lionheart, George Washington, and the messenger Guy Ballard.

Clearly Mary and Elizabeth had some karma together. However, it apparently wasn't necessary for them to meet physically in order to work out that karma. Annice knew of Mrs. Ballard but never contacted her in the flesh. Each of them worked tirelessly for the ascended masters in her own allotted field of service, and perhaps that service itself, as well as their calls to the violet flame, counted for the balancing of their karma.

The messenger gives an important clue in this story. Students of the ascended masters can sometimes get caught up in their past lives. When the records of a past life are first contacted, the feelings accompanying them can be intense. The key is to let them go. Don't identify with that life. Don't hold on to the feelings or memories. And do the spiritual work until you can see that lifetime as impersonal—like reading a history book.

On another note, it is interesting to juxtapose this instruction from Mother with the previous story. One messenger told Annice to not even do her laundry as the work on the book was so pressing, and the other told her to go to a movie.

Students of the messengers and staff members soon learned that the messenger and the masters could be unpredictable. Some who have set themselves up as critics like to quote examples of this unpredictability and characterize it as capriciousness. But from a divine perspective, it has a purpose.

One of the techniques of Zen Buddhism is its use of the koan—most famously "the sound of one hand clapping." The koan is a logical impossibility, something the outer, reasoning mind cannot comprehend. Only when the student is able to transcend the outer mind and rise in consciousness to the higher mind, where all is One, can he solve the riddle.

Kuthumi, who was embodied as St. Francis, says that the masters use every means available to outwit the human consciousness, which tends to like rules and regulations to follow—a path of performance by rote rather than the Holy Spirit. Thus Kuthumi says:

> The purpose of all we do is your ascension. Understand that in order to rescue your soul, we must outsmart or challenge or even bruise that dweller. And we must cajole and contrive circumstances where the eyes of the soul will be opened and true self-knowledge will be gained and thus right choices be made. The entire purpose of our instruction at Summit University from

the heart of Maitreya is so that you, dear chela, might have at your disposal our standards from the ascended master octaves as you exercise free will for right action —right Word and Work. Understand our motive and tolerate our means, for we must act in the best way possible to reach you swiftly.

Consider always the motive of the ascended masters in any adversity, any clash with a chela or family, any misunderstanding of our teaching or the messenger. Consider the motive and consider that the most important part of any experience you have is not what is flung your way but your reaction to it. Your reaction is the determination of your place on the ladder of attainment. Your reaction enables us to act or not to act. Your reaction to anything or everything shows us the fruit that has ripened in you from all of our prior teaching and loving and support as well as discipline.

Thus, perceive the sine wave building towards events that produce a thrust which requires from you a response. Observe the response and you will observe the highest hopes and possibilities which now are given room to manifest. It is always well to pause and take a deep breath and to consider, therefore, before you speak and before you decide on a course of action.[16]

On another occasion Annice described an early recall of that same life and other lives:

Before I was in the teachings, in 1947 or 1948, I had a thyroidectomy [the surgical removal of the thyroid gland in the neck]. **In those days you stayed in hospital for ten days.**

After the incision healed and I was home, I felt as if my head would fall off. For more than two months I wore my husband's handkerchief around my neck because I had the craziest feeling that my head would fall off if I didn't wear it. I later found out that I had indeed lost my head [been beheaded] many times in past lives.

At the time that she told me this story, Annice and I were sitting in a restaurant and I was looking across the table at her. She was wearing a polo-neck sweater: she often wore high necklines to cover the scars from her thyroid surgery and later cardiac surgery. It occurred to me that the sweater looked quite like a ruffle around her neck, and I could easily imagine her in the clothes of those former years. Sometimes God gives us flashes of a past life as we look at one another.

On another occasion, Annice and I had been to one of our lunch meetings at Mammoth Hot Springs restaurant. It was raining hard when we were in the restaurant. The waiter was fascinated with the ruby and amethyst rings that she wore. So Annice showed him the ring with a very large amethyst that she wore on a chain around her neck. Mother wore it while writing *Climb the Highest Mountain,* and it had been given to Annice when Mother retired. We explained to the waiter that amethyst was the stone of transformation.

On the way home Annice asked me to stop so that she could buy some grapes and a few things at the supermarket. Outside there was a little tent filled with spring plants and seedlings, and she purchased some to plant in the garden outside her little home with the white picket fence.

By the time we returned home the rain had stopped and the sun was shining. She was so happy with the lettuces and

Annice relaxing in a corner of her garden
with the white picket fence.

strawberry plants she had bought. She delighted in the green grass, the bright yellow dandelions and the flowers that were blooming in her garden beds. She clapped her hands like a little girl and exclaimed, "More pretty posies!"—such an English term. It reminded me again of Mary, Queen of Scots.

Like the messenger and a number of other chelas, Annice had been a queen in a number of her lifetimes. She said she had "queen's karma," which meant that she needed to serve and work with large groups of people and even groups from other nations to balance that karma. God provided the opportunities that she needed to serve.

Caregiver for Tatiana

During my first three years on staff I kept traveling back and forth between Santa Barbara and Colorado Springs. Starting in 1970, every alternate conference was at Colorado Springs.

In February 1972, I returned to Colorado Springs. Mother had just given birth to Tatiana, and she was three weeks old. I went up to the Tower to visit Mother and her baby.

Mother said, "Here's my baby. Do you want to hold her?" At that time there was a strict rule that no one but the parents could hold a baby up to the age of three months.

"Do you mean I can hold Tatiana?"

"Absolutely.... Ooohhhh, Morya says that you're my babysitter."

"What do you mean?"

"I have been asking Morya for help because I need to write the books, and Morya just said that you are the babysitter. Morya says that this is what you are to do."

"Do you mean that I do this on staff?"

"Yes, but you can still help me with the book [*Climb the Highest Mountain*]."

"Well, Mother, it's been twenty-five years since I had a baby. You must tell me specifically how you would like her cared for."

And that is what I did.

One day up in the nursery, I was playing with Tatiana and Mother came in and said to me, "This is wonderful. This is the little girl that you have always prayed for. Morya said that he is so glad that he can fulfill your wishes."

Mother and I had an understanding. She worked undisturbed except if Tatiana needed her or needed to be nursed. This arrangement worked well most of the time. Then one day I could not settle Tatiana and she needed her mother. I took her to Mother and said, "I think that Tatiana needs you." Then I left and said that I would be in my room when Mother needed me.

I went to my room and thought about the dirty diaper, and so I went down to the laundry to wash it. In the meantime, Mother had wanted to return Tatiana to my care, but I was nowhere to be found. When I was finally located and I returned to her, she said, "Take this child. She is not hungry. I looked all over for you. Where were you?"

I told Mother that I was in the laundry washing the dirty diaper.

This was the time when Mother had begun to do the planetary clearances. She then told me, "You have interrupted me from giving a planetary clearance. You now have the karma of interrupting the clearance of the planet. Instead of being in your room as you said you would be, you were downstairs washing a diaper. Archangel Michael said that your rationalization is why you had to live in California all those years."

That was the end of it. She never would tell me what I had done to Archangel Michael way back.

From this experience, which may sound strange to someone who is not a chela, I learned lessons about obedience and rationalization. It is important to keep your post and to be where you say you will be. The masters need us to keep our post and they rely upon it. Whether it is keeping the promises that we make for a certain set of decrees or to be at our services when we say we will, a promise is a promise. If we make a promise we must keep it and not change our mind, thinking that we have a different reason or a better reason to not do what we have been asked to do.

The masters and the angels are on time and expect us to be there when we say we will be there. A world may depend upon it. And for doing something that is seemingly important, rather than what is asked of us, we can disrupt the plans of the Brotherhood.

Morya says that obedience is better than sacrifice. It is better to be obedient to the master and to do what is required and asked of us rather than be disobedient and try to make up for it later.

Rationalization is the means that the carnal mind has of telling us the alternative to the path that the masters have set before us. The carnal mind says, "Well, you really do not need to do this or that," and it gives us the reasons why.

Mark said I was an old soul and I had been around a long time.

This was another important lesson for Annice—and again, it involved going to the laundry.

Mother was not upset that she had brought Tatiana to her. She was upset because Annice had said she would be in a certain place and she was not there when Mother needed her. Annice could have left a message or a note letting the messenger know where she had gone, but she did not. She could have just stayed where she was and washed the diaper later, but she did not.

This episode shows how seemingly small decisions may have larger consequences on the world scene. The masters have told us that continents and nations and even civilizations have been lost through of a series of small compromises. In this case Annice's seemingly small decision interrupted the spiritual work of the messenger in her calls for the clearance of forces of darkness from the planet.

In our own lives, there may be things that the masters depend on us for. We, too, may be hampering the work of an ascended master when we do not keep our commitments. And the tragedy is that we may not even be aware of it. Annice was fortunate to have the messengers there physically to tell her when she had let the Brotherhood down. But even without a messenger to physically tell us when we have fallen short of the mark, the masters have ways of getting the message to us—if we are sensitive to their impartations.

We don't want to get superstitious about these things or continually second-guess ourselves when things do not go the way we think that they should, but it is healthy to have a realistic self-assessment from time to time, without falling into self-condemnation. This example from Annice's path gives us a sense of co-measurement of what the masters set as a standard for those who would be their chelas.

Annice mentions that Mark told her she was an old soul. Perhaps she had been around the planet long enough that she should have known better! But of course, if we all knew better and did better, we would have ascended long ago.

The connection with California is interesting. The west

coast of the United States was part of the ancient continent of Lemuria. So this statement by Archangel Michael may point to an ancient karma. There are no accidents in the circumstances where we find ourselves, and it is often the equation of karma that brings us back to certain places.

This story also illustrates the trust that Mother and Morya had in Annice in asking her to babysit for Tatiana. When a child is born, the bones of the skull are still growing and there are two soft spots (fontanelles) where the bones have not yet joined together. These are at the top of the head, corresponding to the crown chakra. One soft spot stays open for several years, one closes after several months. While the fontanelles are open the child is also open spiritually and subject to the vibration of those who physically contact it, and it is up to the parents to protect the baby's aura and forcefield.

Therefore the masters and the messenger recommend we only allow immediate family or those whose vibration we trust to handle a newborn in those first few formative months. For a similar reason, it is better not to take a baby out in public unnecessarily in the first few months.

Couples were also advised not to tell people about a pregnancy until it shows—four to five months for the first pregnancy and a little earlier for subsequent ones. This is to guard the alchemy of the early formation of the child in the womb.

Before the Karmic Board

One story from La Tourelle illustrates the closeness of Annice and Mother, what was at times almost a mother-daughter relationship. It also shows Annice's ability to stand for what she believed to be right, even when others disagreed.

At La Tourelle, Mother had almost no money to call her own. Finances were tight for our little organization, but a staff member had inherited some money and he would go downtown with Mother and buy furnishings for her that she picked out. It was the first time in her life that she had been able to spend any money at all on furnishings, and she was able to furnish the Tower at La Tourelle. Eventually Mark told her that she was not to buy any more antiques and that there was to be an end to it.

One day Mother came home with a lovely emerald glass carafe. It was about fourteen inches high and made of antique glass, and she was just thrilled with it. Someone went to Mark and told him that Elizabeth was buying more antiques after he had told her not to. Mark called a meeting in his office with four senior staff members, myself, and of course Mother.

The meeting had a very serious vibration to it. When I entered the room it felt to me as if the Karmic Board was present. Mother felt the presence too, and she was very concerned that she had done something wrong.

Mark said that this was indeed a matter before the Karmic Board. He said that Elizabeth had been devious, underhanded, disobedient and rebellious. I thought to myself, "Thank God it's not me!" Mark said that each one of those present would have the opportunity to say something before the Karmic Board made their decision about the matter.

Everyone had their say, and they all spoke against Mother. Finally I had the opportunity to speak. I said, "Well, Mark, perhaps you don't understand the heart of a woman. You have your CB radios and cameras, and eight or ten pairs of eyeglasses, and yet Elizabeth has very few things. As far as I am concerned she is very circumspect and careful. Occasionally a woman just needs something lovely for her soul. Mark, you do not check with her when you purchase something that you want. I see no great crime here."

After everyone had spoken, Mark conferred with the Karmic Board. The end result was that Mother was forgiven for her supposed crime. Later Mother embraced me in her dressing room and said, "If ever I needed a mother you are it! My own mother could not fulfill her spiritual office, and you are my mother."

Several other times later she said, "If ever I needed a mother I've got one. You are my mother."

This is a profound personal story about the relationship between Mother and Annice. It also provides an interesting insight into the path and how the masters view the tests of life.

Mother was subject to very strict disciplines in her training as a messenger. Morya had dealt with a number of female chelas and messengers in earlier years who had turned into prima donnas, and he was determined Mother would not go down the same path. He wasn't going to put up with any human nonsense.

Here was a situation where Mother had disobeyed a direct order from Mark. No one is above the law, not even a messenger, and it seems that the situation was serious enough to warrant the involvement of the Karmic Board.

For whatever reason, the staff members who were there took a hard line on the situation. It was true that she had been disobedient, but it is wise to remember that there are two sides to every story, and the motive of the heart is important.

Annice took a position that was different from everyone else. This must have taken some courage. It takes a certain strength to know one's own mind and heart and to be able to stand for what you believe is right, even when everyone else sees things differently.

Mother once said that it was the ascended lady master Portia who stepped forward to deliver the verdict of the Karmic Board in this case. She is known as the Goddess of Justice, and she explained the perspective of the Karmic Board as to justice in this case. Portia said that against the backdrop of thousands of years of Mother's service to the Brotherhood, this incident was a peccadillo.

Did the input from a sincere soul such as Annice make the difference? We do not know. Kuan Yin has spoken of her own advocacy for souls before the Karmic Board, pleading for mercy for those who come before the bar of cosmic justice. Perhaps Annice was performing a similar role in this case. Anyone who knows Annice might find this surprising, since she is known for her white-ray personality and her strict sense of discipline. But Annice also understood the human condition—

we occupy human bodies and are subject to the weaknesses of the flesh, or even simple human needs.

Annice says that the presence of the Karmic Board was tangible in the room, and it is interesting that they wanted to hear from everyone present before making their decision. No doubt the opinions and recommendations of these unascended chelas were taken into account in their deliberations, but possibly the Karmic Board also wanted to have an understanding of where these chelas were in consciousness. The chelas themselves also had the opportunity to see how their own sense of justice and mercy aligned with the higher perspective of the Karmic Board.

One thing we might learn from this story is that our daily actions are important to the Karmic Board, and these masters may be far more involved in our day-to-day lives than we realize. Not in a psychic or superstitious sense, but in a very real way we may have a relationship with these great beings of light. One way we do this is through the letters and petitions we write to them each year.

We can also learn that God and the masters are merciful. They do not always see things as we do, and they look to the quality of the heart. Their decision and their reasoning in this case helps us to get beyond the false concept of a wrathful God that has come down to us from a sometimes distorted Christianity and from the false gods of the Nephilim. We see a justice that is a comfort to our minds and hearts and souls.

One wonders what Mark knew or did not know as he conducted this inquiry. Perhaps it was a significant initiation for everyone involved, including Mark, Mother and those who judged her. No doubt there were deep lessons for all.

Mark's Voice

Often at the end of a class Mark was tired and his voice got hoarse. Sometimes he would come in with a purple silk scarf around his neck, one that he had acquired in Darjeeling. And when we saw that scarf we knew we were in for a treat.

Mark would read a poem when his voice was too tired to give a lecture. He would ask Tom Miller to go and get the copy of Longfellow's poems from his study. Mark had embodied as Longfellow, and it was always a perfect end to a perfect conference when Mark read his poetry in his beautiful, rich voice.

After Mark's ascension, Mother and I went to a spa and we were both swimming in the pool. "Listen to this," said Mother, "Mark is singing to me." Mother could hear Mark singing to her in the spa. He was taking singing lessons right after his ascension so that he could be a better singer. Mark loved to sing.

Mark Prophet loved to sing, but he never had the opportunity to take formal training during his life. The Ascended Lady Master Nada Rayborn, who was an opera singer in her final embodiment, once spoke of the training in singing she offers to newly ascended masters. She explained that we take our positive momentums with us when we ascend, and with a perfect body, without the burdens and limitations of the physical plane, we can make rapid progress in those areas that may have been challenging for us when we were in embodiment. However, attainment is not automatic, even after the ascension, and we continue to receive training from those who have greater mastery in those areas where we wish to advance.

Mother once said that she knew that Mark would go to Nada Rayborn for voice training after his ascension. And when Mark was ready, he came to Mother, with an orchestra and a choir of angels, to sing a song of his love for his twin flame.

Mother spoke a number of times of her love of playing the piano when she was a teenager. But when she became a messenger she gave this up, along with knitting and embroidery, to focus on her world service. She said that as we devote our lives to the ascended masters for the saving of the planet, we may have to postpone some things that are of lesser importance for the sake of the mission. She said, "I'll do them after I ascend."

Mother worked very hard during her life, but, she also took time for recreation and balance. And in the midst of the battle of Armageddon, she said that her rest and recreation were often when she traveled to the etheric retreats of the masters during sleep and experienced there great art, beauty and music and the true re-creation of the soul.

Each of us must find that point of balance in our own life. We can be kind to our four lower bodies and provide them with the necessary elements for their health and service, but without indulging in entertainment at the expense of our mission. This is the path of the middle way.

Knowing Mother

At the time that I joined staff in 1969, I was forty-nine and one of the youngest staff members. Almost everyone else was older than me, except for Mother, who was twenty-nine.

No one really knows Mother who did not go through those days with her when Mark was first gone. Mother was thirty-three when Mark passed on in 1973 (she was born in 1939). To really understand Mother, you had to be there with her when she lost Mark.

When Mark was here, he ran the whole organization. He poked his nose into everything and knew every single thing that was going on. Nothing escaped his attention. He would go down to the mailroom at night to open the letters, read the mail and see how much money had come in to meet the bills and to publish the Word.

Mother was strictly in the background. She was Mrs. Prophet and mother of the children. At conferences she would give one lecture and deliver one dictation and Mark did all the rest. She spent much of her time in the Tower at La Tourelle writing *Climb the Highest Mountain*. When Mark left, all that he had formerly done, including the administration of the organization, immediately fell upon her. All of this was completely unknown to her.

At the same time, several young men who had recently

joined the staff were vying for her attention, even trying to marry her and to take over the organization. She had to fend them off.

No one knows how difficult it was to make a complete switch from Mrs. Prophet, wife and mother, to Elizabeth Clare Prophet, messenger and leader of The Summit Lighthouse.

This was a period of complete change in lifestyle for Mother. She had to conquer her feelings of inadequacy, and unless people realize the difficult time she had in those days, they do not really know her. She was now messenger, CEO of The Summit Lighthouse and eventually Church Universal and Triumphant [which was founded on May 1, 1975]. She was a young woman, and suddenly the karma and responsibility of the whole planet was thrust upon her. This burden continued for many years.

Mark had left when he was fifty-four, and Mother was not intended to have the whole weight of the planet upon her. Mark told me that the plan was that two of the children, Sean and Tatiana, were intended to become the next messengers. But clearly they decided otherwise.

One day Elizabeth came to me (we did not yet call her Mother at that time) and she said, "Annice, you are going to have to take care of the staff. I can't stand it. There is just too much for me to do. I'll do the dictations and the classes, and you'll have to care for the staff and the Motherhouse."

Seeing Mother on the platform, with the mantle of the ascended masters on her and in the light of their presence so tangible, it might be easy to think that her victory was quite secure and that she didn't face the kinds of difficulties that the rest of us encounter—or if she did have to deal with them, that somehow the masters' assistance made it easier. But of course, this was never the case. The masters have said many times that there are no favorite sons. The messenger was no exception.

In fact, the challenges she faced required supreme determination. In 1973 Mother told her staff that her divine plan was originally that she would not become a messenger until the age of thirty-three, her age when Mark passed. The timetable was accelerated when she went to the roof of her apartment building in Boston and made the fiat, "Saint Germain, you've got to come and get me now! I can't wait any longer!"

The masters answered this call immediately and arranged within a few days for Mark Prophet to go to Boston. Mother met him there and her training as a messenger began. But as a result of this acceleration of her timetable, she had a very intense period of initiation. In a few short years she had to go through a process of purging—mental, emotional and physical —that would otherwise have taken ten years. In order to get through this, she had to summon all of her will and determination. It was also a painful process at times, like going through surgery.

Then, when Mark left, she faced what was perhaps an even greater challenge—having to shoulder the whole burden of the activity alone. Some saw this as an opportunity to gain power for themselves rather than an opportunity to help her bear the burden. Fortunately Annice was one of those who were there, like Simon the Cyrenian, to help Mother bear her cross during this difficult time.

Annice had a balanced view of Mother. She knew her as the Guru and the representative of the masters, but she also knew her as a human being, in one sense a fellow chela also striving on the path. Unlike many others, she did not have an idolatry of Mother, thinking that she was somehow the embodiment of perfection. Rather, she honored the mantle and office that Mother wore and was willing to receive the disciplines of chelaship from someone who was apparently imperfect.

Annice and I talked about her relationship with the messenger and how it has changed since the messenger has retired and gone into seclusion. Annice commented:

It is still possible to have a relationship with Mother at inner levels, but people today miss the warmth of the personal interchange and the give-and-take of the Guru-chela relationship.

In the olden days you had to live with the Guru to understand the Guru. I have been privileged to have lived in the same house as both messengers, Mark and Mother. I believe that those of us who knew Mark and Mother were meant to teach others. Unfortunately most of those who could have trained others have left, been edged out or had to leave. Also it appears that some people today are not so willing to take instruction from others or from someone who is not a messenger but who has been trained by one.

To have been a part of the small circle of chelas with Mark at La Tourelle or at Santa Barbara was a priceless opportunity. We think of the home in Bethany where Jesus taught Mary, Martha, Lazarus and the apostles. The masters have described that home as the first teaching center.

In later years, after Mark's ascension, when the staff numbered hundreds rather than dozens, the experience was different. Few of the staff had regular personal interaction with the messenger apart from those who assisted her with her work. But for all who were in the community, it was still a very special time. They would see Mother as she regularly preached, delivered dictations and lead decree sessions. At social occasions or just in day-to-day life, staff might also meet her in the way and interact. There was a tangible sense of the masters leading the community and directing its work.

Sometimes those who were not there have an unrealistic sense of what it was like, just as they might have a rose-tinted view of what life would have been like with Jesus. People might think how wonderful it would have been to be there with him, to bask in his love and light. But there must have been times when Jesus and the apostles were all cold, wet and hungry. They had to walk everywhere and they must have been weary at times. Sometimes they were in fear for their lives. And sometimes the apostles were out of alignment and Jesus rebuked them sternly.

Mother spoke a number of times of people who never met Mark Prophet who imagine how wonderful it would have been to know him—some of them would not have liked the real Mark Prophet at all. He was open, he was direct, he was unpredictable, he could be stern and uncompromising with people's indulgences, he could be out of sorts when dealing with the burdens of his office.

Some people were offended when their human consciousness was exposed. Some were offended when he did not fit the mold of how they thought a messenger should behave. But for those who could see beyond the outer, life with Mark was an opportunity to know someone who was very close to God, a true twentieth-century adept.

On a number of occasions the masters have spoken of their desire that those who received training in chelaship directly from the messengers should pass that training on to others. When she was serving on the staff under Mother, Annice did exactly this in her many roles and assignments, both at headquarters and in teaching centers. Some chelas took this well, learning a great deal from her about the path. Some rejected what she had to offer.

Perhaps it is not surprising to see the same thing today. And yet Annice was disappointed, and no doubt the masters have been also, to see that the type of training in chelaship that she received has often not been welcomed after the messenger's retirement. The masters have spoken of the folly of those who were unwilling to take instruction from anyone but a messenger. They miss out on many opportunities for self-correction and progress on the path. El Morya has said:

> Remember this and listen well: If you can't get along with or serve your fellowman or your fellow chela on the path, then you won't get along with or serve the Ascended Masters. And so we withdraw from those who call themselves chelas but who fail in their service to and with each other.
>
> Then there is always the chela who says sanctimoniously to another chela on the path, "Well, I love your Christ Self, but I can't stand your human." They presuppose that they understand which is which. They look at the chela and they see the human. I say, look again and behold in his place the Master who declared, "Inasmuch as ye have done it unto one of the least of these my brethren, ye have done it unto me."
>
> Can you look at me squarely in the eye and tell me that you always know when the human consciousness is acting and when it is the Master working through a

fellow chela to test the threshold of your pride, your irritation? We do not need to appear to the chela to test his soul. We have only to use another chela to determine what is the level of sacrifice. How much of the self are you willing to surrender in order to retain the privilege of working side by side with those whose devotion to our flame may be far beyond your own?[17]

Remember Morya's famous injunction, "If the messenger be an ant, heed him!"

There were a number of times throughout the years, beginning in the 1970s, when Mother was offered the choice of taking her ascension or remaining in embodiment. We can see the choice that she made. It must surely have been a sacrifice, but she decided to stay and to stay again. Her children chose not to take up the opportunity to become messengers or carry on the mission. Again, free will is paramount.

One can only imagine how difficult it must have been to be the child of a messenger in a close-knit community. One burden they faced was the very expectation of their future mission and the fact that people sometimes treated them differently because they were children of the messengers.

As far as we know, Mother and the masters did not anoint a messenger to follow in her footsteps when she leaves embodiment, but this does not mean that God might not raise up another at a future time, and the church's articles of incorporation provide a mechanism by which a future messenger could be recognized. Mother once said she did not plan to designate a successor because when and if the time came, God would raise someone up.

The Cyclopea Marathon

The fifth ray is the ray of healing, truth, precipitation and vision. Cyclopea is the Elohim of this ray, a great Cosmic Being who radiates these qualities to the earth. His decree is number 50.05 in the Summit Lighthouse decree book, a prayer for divine vision and to reveal the truth or the error of any situation. It is also used to bring abundance and supply, which are qualities of the fifth ray. Annice and Mother once had a very interesting experience with this decree.

In 1974 we were having problems in Santa Barbara. None of the problems were from within, such as we have now. They were all from without. There were problems with the neighbors who hated us, zoning issues. Mark had just ascended and left us, and Mother was adjusting to moving from being the wife and mother of their four children to being the messenger and in charge of the entire organization. We were also dealing with witchcraft and black magic in the cities of Los Angeles and Santa Barbara, and there were problems with money and income.

Mother told me one day that Morya wanted a Cyclopea marathon. No one had any idea of exactly what that was, but Mother said, "We have the Will of God Focus [a small chapel on the grounds of the Motherhouse] and we can gather everyone and do a twenty-four hour decree vigil to Cyclopea with people taking turns around the clock."

Summit University was in session at the time, so that's what we did. We gave a twenty-four hour marathon to Cyclopea. We just did Cyclopea decrees around the clock and nothing else.

The next day we could hardly move. Mother called me and asked, "Annice, how do you feel?"

"Terrible!"

Mother said, "I can hardly stand up."

I told Mother, "I don't think the twenty-four hours of decrees to Cyclopea was a good idea. Something is not right."

Mother said, "I'll ask Morya."

Morya told her, "My dear, never do Cyclopeas without following up with violet flame. Cyclopeas will expose evil and will bring problems to your awareness, but you must do the violet flame to clear up what has been exposed."

We all live and learn on the path! And in this case, Mother and Annice found out through experience that there is a right way and a wrong way to do a Cyclopea marathon. But in spite of not having the best strategy, Mother said that this marathon was instrumental in bringing about the exposure of the Watergate conspiracy and the illegal activities in the Nixon White House. Morya apparently did not tell Mother the intended purpose of the marathon, but she was obedient to his direction and the purpose was achieved.

The Cyclopea decree will expose problems and bring them to the surface. What is hidden becomes revealed, but what Annice and Mother found out is that it cannot be left there. The darkness that is revealed needs to be dealt with—through judgment calls, transmutation, Astreas, and whatever else is needed to clean it up. Untransmuted energy was what was making Annice and Mother feel so terrible. They were obedient to the Master's directive but they suffered because they had not thought through the consequences of what they were doing and had not thought to ask.

We have learned a lot since then. Mother has directed many marathons, including Cyclopea marathons. She has given instruction to decree leaders and demonstrated the science of directing decrees for focused purposes. For example, when we give a large block of decrees to Cyclopea, we precede it with decrees for protection and we follow up with violet flame decrees (and Judgment Calls and decrees to Astrea if there is time) to clean up and transmute what has been exposed.

Under Mother's direction, Annice and her staff at the Office of Ministry a number of years ago published a Services Manual outlining how to conduct a variety of decree sessions and services for those who are more experienced in decrees and also for new students. This manual contains much valuable instruction on how to structure a decree service effectively.

An interesting insight from this story is that some of the teachings we have today came forth through trial and error. The master may give an instruction, but the chela must also use common sense and ask clarifying questions if necessary. Similarly, when Mother gave instructions to staff, they were expected to carry out those instructions as given, but they were also expected to apply what they had learned previously and not simply robotically carry out an action without thinking about the consequences. If something was not clear, they were expected to ask, and not unilaterally decide to do it differently.

Annice and Mother

Annice spoke a number of times about her relationship with Mother. Here are two snippets:

Mother and I had a normal relationship. We were always just girls together. I would not even know how to write a book about her. All I could do was to write a book about Mark and call it *Memories of Mark*.

I can't write a nice little book like the one that Evelyn Dykman wrote [*Sweet Mystery of Life*]. Too many things happened, and mine was a more down-to-earth story. Mother said that I was like family.

Only a very few chelas had this kind of relationship with Mother. For a number of those who had a personal relationship, over time it became a case of "familiarity breeds contempt." They saw Mother's human idiosyncrasies and could no longer respect her in the role of messenger and Guru, and most are no longer here.

On the other hand, for many who were devoted chelas it was difficult to simply be a friend to the messenger when she needed a friend. Perhaps this is not so surprising—there are challenges in having a personal friendship with your supervisor in a normal employment situation, but the role of Guru has the added weight of being active twenty-four hours a day. Mother spoke about a certain loneliness that this created for her.

Annice was able to have an everyday relationship with Mother, but also relate to her in the Guru-chela relationship and switch to this when it was necessary. Annice might be in or out of favor from time to time in the chelaship department as she went through the disciplines of the path, but the family relationship continued through these temporary ups and downs.

Annice was comfortable around Mother and Mother could be at ease with her. The following little story illustrates one aspect of this relationship.

When I was working with Mother on *Climb the Highest Mountain*, I was frequently flying back and forth from La Tourelle to Santa Barbara, and I was getting tired.

Mother said to me one day, "You look harried."

I said to her, "I am just tired of telling people what to do. I just want to be a little pussycat snuggled up in a rocking chair, sitting in the sun."

Mother giggled—I had not heard her giggle before. She said, "With so much blue in your aura, it is hard to imagine you as a pussycat."

The Messenger Sees the Electronic Belt

Mark really liked Lester. They were good friends. However, Mother and Lester did not always get along. There were times when he did not like Mother and Mother did not like him.

Lester was, for a period of time, the official photographer for the organization. But there was a problem. Whenever he took Mother's photograph, she always closed her eyes. This happened every time. The result was that the photographs could not be used.

Finally Mother said to me one day, "I can't help it, Annice. I tried. But every time I see him, all I see is his electronic belt."

The Guru can see who we are and who we are not. In some ways this may bring out our worst fears. No one wants to think of the Guru being able to see one's negative aspects. And that is exactly what the electronic belt is—the repository of the darkness that is within us from this and past lives.

The messengers have told us that sometimes God would show them something that they needed to see about one of their students so that they could pray for that one or point out a flaw. But for the most part their preference was to choose not to see these things, even when they could. Instead they would choose to hold the immaculate concept for each chela, the divine image of each one as a perfected being.

In her book *Community,* Mother says, "I love you unconditionally, and I am not sitting and gazing upon your karma, your records, your aura and all of that. I am not interested in that. I am interested in God in you."

Mother and Morya
Train Annice to Be a Writer

One Sunday night in Santa Barbara, Mother called me and said, "Annice, what are you doing?"

"I am lying on a slant board because my back hurts."

"Then I won't come over and see you. I'll just talk on the phone. There has been a big coup at the White Lodge group in Del Mar. I am sure that Morya has arranged it. All of the Board of Directors are Keepers of the Flame and they voted me in to be in charge as the Guardian of the Shrine.

The White Lodge is accustomed to a monthly magazine, so Morya says that we have to write a monthly magazine. Do you know how to write?"

"No! You know what I have done. I have no experience."

"Well, I do not have time to write it and Morya says that you should write it."

"I don't know what to do."

"It should be the teachings of the masters, but initially we should not say too much about them because the White Lodge was a spiritual organization founded by their master Azrael."*

---

* The messenger has explained that Azrael was not an ascended master. He was just a run-of-the-mill disembodied spirit who happened to dictate a series of books through the psychic channel who founded the White Lodge. The teachings in the books by Azrael were basic and introductory, but contained a degree of inaccuracy along with truth.

So I wrote these little booklets and Mother supervised me. Basically what I did was find the teachings from the dictations and lectures and paste them together. Sometimes Mother would come and visit me and say, "What are you doing, cutie? Cutting and pasting like a big jigsaw?"

For the first few months, Mother went over every cotton-picking word. Every single word was approved by her. I followed her around everywhere—even to the hairdresser or to the gym—so that she could check every word of those *Crystallization of the God Flame* booklets. Finally, after six months of her supervising me in every aspect of the work, she said, "This is nonsense. You are doing a beautiful job and you know what you are doing. Just keep doing it. I do not need to see it in this level of detail."

After that, Mother would still review each booklet before it was printed, but not in as much detail as before. One day at the Ashram of the World Mother in Los Angeles (we had moved there by this time) she was approving a booklet on the Maha Chohan, and she said to me, "Morya says that Annice is doing a very nice job of cutting and pasting, but he wants her to write!"

Those were the kinds of messages I got from Morya. He never patted me on the back and said, "You dear sweet soul." No, Morya's comments to me were always instruction or correction that furthered my spiritual growth.

I said to Mother, "Tell Morya I never took writing in college. I majored in Latin and French."

Can you imagine the answer that I got back?

Morya said, "Tell Annice that she didn't write in Latin or French either!"

I could have crawled under the table.

To this day I do not know if I wrote dirty books on Atlantis or if I just refused to write. But clearly the master wanted me to write to fulfill my divine plan and to complete a mission begun long ago.

Morya was absolutely right. I never wrote anything. I simply cut and pasted and wove things together seamlessly. Every *God Flame* booklet at that time was a miracle of co-ordination. The sentences were put together from various sources and they fit together with absolute perfection. I did not even have to add a "but" or an "and."

Each *Crystallization of the God Flame* contained teachings on a particular ray. So with the fourth ray and the master Serapis Bey, I started writing my own words.

Mother told me that in these particular publications it was perfectly fine for me to present the masters' teaching in my own words without quoting them directly. She reviewed the one on Serapis Bey and said, "You have done a beautiful job." She also added one paragraph to the booklet. I told her, "What do you want to take out?"

She said, "What do you mean?"

I explained that the booklet was limited to sixteen pages, and if one paragraph was added another would have to be taken out, since we were at the limit. She said, "Well, fine! Take mine out. I like yours better."

There were about six more of these booklets published after this, and then we stopped producing them. Here's why.

I wrote them once a month and we sent them out to a subscription list. During those years I traveled from Santa Barbara to San Francisco to La Tourelle taking the *God Flame* work with me wherever I went. I had typesetters in each location and the booklets were printed in Santa Barbara. The booklets contained teachings about the various masters. My plan was to go through the seven chohans and then the seven archangels and then the seven Elohim. I got through the chohans and was half way through the archangels when Mother called me again to talk to her. By this time I was in charge of the Office of Ministry. We called it ONC at that time [Office of the National Coordinator].

Mother said, "Annice, I want you to go to London tomorrow. I need you to dismiss a study group leader."

"Mother, I would be glad to go but I have not finished my *God Flame* for this month."

"Well, your travels take precedence."

And that was the last *God Flame* I ever did.

Thank goodness many of the teachings that the *God Flames* contained are now available in the book *The Masters and Their Retreats.*

A sudden change of assignment from the masters or the messenger was something that could happen at any time for those serving on the staff. Annice was obedient and dropped the project to do the next assignment. It then became apparent that the first assignment was over. That was life with the messengers. Annice knew that projects started might not necessarily be finished or that a project could evolve or change into something else.

This story illustrates how important a sense of timing is in the work for the masters. The masters teach us that there is often a certain cycle or period of time for a particular project, and if the task is not completed in the appointed time it is much more difficult, or even impossible, to take it up again later. It is almost as if the cycle or the wave of energy for that task has moved on. Lanello says:

> There are many things in the duties of the day that cannot be postponed to the next, for when they are postponed and the momentum wanes, so often the cycle is lost and the project is not completed. And how difficult it is to get that project done when you have to crank it up again and start all over! So understand that this is life—life that is measured by the soul and the heart and the Holy Christ Self.[18]

Annice was always a finisher. She liked to complete every task she was given. I think it was hard for her not to have completed the series on the archangels in the *Crystallization of the God Flame* magazines. She kept the notes for years in a file drawer in her office. The finisher in Annice felt great satisfaction in being able to incorporate that information into *The Masters and Their Retreats*.

An interesting side note to this story is that Annice was told to go to London to perform a difficult and unpleasant task, to dismiss the leader of the group there. This is not a decision that the messenger would have taken lightly or without a very good reason.

On occasions when such actions were taken, it often caused some turmoil in a group. Yet the decision was made not only for the good of the community, but also, ultimately, for the good of the individual soul. When other means had been tried and not resulted in a necessary correction, strong action might be the only hope to awaken the soul to an out-of-alignment state and to rescue that one from making more karma.

People often did not realize that Annice was working under the messenger's direction in performing these difficult tasks. The messenger trusted her and trained her in how to handle these situations. Often she had to deliver a specific message to the other party and to deliver it with the flame, the vibration and the energy of the master and the full office of the mantle of messenger. She was frequently instructed to deliver the message exactly as it was given and not to soften the blow.

People who were on the receiving end of such disciplines sometimes reacted with anger and even hatred of Annice personally. Unfortunately, these people did not perceive the master's hand working through events. They missed the chance to receive the discipline and to use it as a spur to make very necessary changes in their lives. Annice directly bore the burden of this reaction, and she bore it willingly for the sake of the masters and the mission.

An Afternoon Nap

On many occasions on the way out of a restaurant or returning from errands, Annice would say to me, "Time to take a nap." I would then take her home, and off she went to sleep.

All of Annice's friends knew that she took a nap every day from about 1:30 to 4 P.M. She put in a very full week, however, often working into the evening and on weekends.

One time Annice told me how she began her habit of an afternoon nap.

Helen MacDonald told me about napping. She had a PhD, and yet was cooking the meals for the staff. Helen would go for a nap in the afternoon after lunch. She undressed and even took off her girdle to completely relax.

I thought this was nonsense until the day that another staff member tried to choke me. I was meeting with him and two other male staff members when he asked for some money for a project. He said that he had to have it, but I refused as there was no budget for it and no funds. He asked again, and again I refused. Then he came around from behind his desk and grabbed me by the throat. I fended him off with the help of the others and made a hasty exit in my car.

I could not sleep all that night. The next day Mother asked

me, "What's wrong?" After I said I could not sleep, Mother wanted to know why, so I told her what had happened.

She explained that I could not sleep because my poor body elemental was shook up and because it was not safe for me to leave my body when this person was so angry, so my Holy Christ Self would not let me sleep. She told me to go to her room and take a nap. When I got home Helen MacDonald asked the same questions and insisted that I take a nap.

From time to time after that Mother would ask me if I was taking a nap. Years later, in the 1990s, when we were working on publications up near Mother's home at the Inner Retreat, she insisted that I come up to her own home and sleep in her bed for my afternoon nap. She did not want me just resting on a foldaway cot. So I did just that for almost a year, walking over to Mother's house and back in the afternoons.

Apart from the physical benefits, sometimes a short nap can be a way to leave your body for a time, to de-stress and recharge in the octaves of light. Perhaps this was what Annice was doing with her naps.

The messenger had her own way of doing this. She lived with the condition of petit mal epilepsy since childhood. On one occasion she spoke of this condition as being absent from her body for brief intervals as a means of release from the burdens of the world. It was a means of entering in to the octaves of light for microscopic periods.

For the Judgment

Over the decades of the history of The Summit Lighthouse, many people have come and gone. A few of these have become vocal critics of the messengers and the organization. This has even included those who were in senior positions, who worked closely with Mark and Mother.

I was discussing this with Annice one day, wondering why we experienced these repeated betrayals by those we had considered friends and fellow-chelas. Annice told me of a conversation she once had with Mother.

One day I said to Mother, "Mother, why are so many around you causing so much trouble?"

She said, "Dear, I have told you before. I took embodiment for the judgment." She said this twice.

Long ago, in the hour of the fallen angels' rebellion against God, the masters have told us that the messenger, at that time holding an office in the angelic hierarchy, volunteered to take embodiment to persuade them to return to God's service and also to counteract the darkness they would inflict upon the children of God. Alpha and Omega granted this request and explained that during certain cycles of opportunity, she would be with these fallen angels as their mother. At the end of those cycles, if they had not turned to serve the light, she would be their judge.

Some of those very fallen angels have walked the halls of The Summit Lighthouse and Summit University and served on the staff. The messenger's assignment was to serve them, give them the teaching, extend God's love to them, help them balance their karma, and give them the vision of life in God's service. Some responded. Some of them, however, turned against the messengers and the masters.

It was often a shock to see this happen, in some cases almost overnight. But this was a part of the process of the working out of God's judgment, the separation of light and darkness. These individuals had to be brought to the place where they were before their original rebellion against God, with a measure of karma balanced, knowing the teaching and the path are true, knowing God's love and forgiveness and having the vision of his kingdom. It was almost astounding to see that some of them, knowing all this, made the very same decision that they had made, millions of years ago, to turn against God in anger and rebellion.

Not long after her retirement, Mother said, "Don't be moved. Morya is in charge. People are making their choices."

The Weight of the World

This picture of Annice carrying a globe of the world was taken in 1978 during the ceremony in which our headquarters was moved from a rented campus in Pasadena to Camelot, a 218-acre property in the Santa Monica Mountains behind Malibu. Annice once told me the story behind this picture, which reveals as much about the messenger as it does about Annice.

This picture was taken when we moved from Pasadena to Camelot. Various members of the staff were given holy focuses from the altar in Pasadena to carry to the chapel at Camelot. We carried these focuses, including statues, pictures and crystals, through the gates of Camelot, down the long driveway, over the bridge at Swan Lake, through the arch, across Excalibur Square, up the steps and down the aisle of the new chapel, which we had named the Chapel of the Holy Grail.

People were bringing the focuses one by one, and Mother was accepting them and placing them on the new altar. Everyone had been given something to carry. I had the globe of the world which had been on the altar at Pasadena.

An amazing thing happened. As I carried the globe, it got heavier and heavier, until I was almost staggering. I felt that I was literally carrying the world. When Mother saw me bearing the globe she came down from the altar and took it from me saying, "Is it getting too heavy, dear? You can give it to me. You have carried it long enough. I'll take it from here."

The messengers' role is to hold the balance for world karma. I knew that for a short period of time in carrying the globe I got to feel a little bit of the weight of world karma that the messengers bear. I was glad to hand the world back to the messenger, who had the mantle to carry it. I knew that Mother was taking it from me again.

A Book for Every Conference

Mother was meeting with some of her senior staff around the dining room table at her home at Broad Beach, near Camelot. Seven of us were present, and we were talking about editorial projects.

Jesus spoke to Mother and said, "I wish you would make a book of each one of the conferences. We [the Great White Brotherhood] have given each of them as a spiral and a matrix."

I took Jesus at his word and edited all the lectures and dictations from one conference. I had it all ready to go. But one staff member said to Mother, "That's Mickey Mouse stuff! No one will read that!" And so the project went nowhere.

When the masters and the messengers are working with chelas in embodiment, they are always dealing with the equation of free will. The masters may give an instruction, but it is up to the chela to carry it out. The encouragement or discouragement of a chela or staff member could affect the outcome of a project or even the decision of the messenger.

Mother once spoke of a situation in a particular city where the masters had called for the establishment of a teaching center. The students there were not doing what the masters had called for, and they had various reasons why they couldn't, or wouldn't. Mother explained that she could go there, be very stern with them, and demand that they fulfill the masters' request. They would probably do so, but it would be reluctantly, and they would probably sabotage the project subconsciously and make it fail, proving that they were right all along. So she respected their free will and left them to their own devices.

The masters respect free will and do not often interfere with the free will choices of their students. It is sobering responsibility to realize how much the masters are dependent on us and how much control we have over what they can accomplish in this plane.

The master did not give a timeline for his project of publishing a book for each conference, and it could still be done as a future publishing project. Annice often said that she would love to see a book based on the Retreat on the Ascension, the outstanding seminar conducted by the messenger in San Francisco in August 1979. When the masters plan a conference, they see multiple uses for the material and begin with the end in mind.

A Center in Paris

I once tried to start a teaching center in Paris. The masters had called for Teaching Centers in Paris and Rome. I was in Camelot at ONC at the time when the instruction was given. Immediately I packed my suitcase and went to France determined to start a teaching center there. Before I left I checked the membership list and discovered that there was not a single Keeper of the Flame living in Paris.

When I arrived, I went to the US Embassy. I asked them, "How do I rent an apartment in Paris?" They told me that I could not rent an apartment as I could only have a visa to stay in the country for three months. One needed to have residency to rent an apartment in Paris. This was not going to work. I tried everything I could think of, but in the end I had to leave Paris without having a center there.

I went to Rome and found the exact same thing. I do not know why we have never had a center in Paris or Rome.

The request to open centers in Paris and Rome was delivered by Jophiel and Christine on January 1, 1981. They said:

Beloved, you who cherish the shrines, the cathedrals, the history, the culture of the Great Divine Director in Europe—open up your hearts! Give your life and your full support in abundant measure. For we would, this very day, open our retreat in Paris if souls of light would offer to be the innkeepers of this shrine of Saint Germain and the Master of Paris. But we begin in Rome—the eternal home of angels, light-bearers. And the citadel of Nephilim.[19]

Annice tried her best to do the master's will, and with the approval of the messenger, she traveled to Paris and Rome to establish centers of light. Yet it seemed that it could not be done at that time. We might wonder why the masters would ask for something that seems to have been impossible to carry out at the time.

One possibility is that there were specific individuals who were destined to fulfill this call of the masters, who had the means to do it but did not respond. I recently found out that there were people living in Italy at that very time who were studying the teachings, but they were not on our mailing list and Annice did not know they were there. Perhaps more spiritual work was needed to cut them free, clear the blocks, and make the necessary connections on the outer.

We don't know all that the masters saw in this situation, but Mother later told her students that the reason it was difficult to establish a center in Paris was because of the records of the French Revolution. Saint Germain had been in France at that time as le Comte de Sainte Germaine, "the Wonderman of Europe," and had been working with the court and the royal family, encouraging reforms and trying to head off the debacle that ensued when his counsel was ignored. The karma of these events was a burden on the people that made it more difficult for the light to be anchored there.

Nothing is in vain, however. Annice was in those cities and made the calls and gave her decrees. One never knows what this action may have forestalled in terms of karmic return or what personal karma or debt to life Annice was able to balance by simply being in the city. Mother was later to reveal to Annice that she and Mother had been embodied together in that city during the French Revolution, as Mother and son—Mother was Marie Antoinette and Annice was her son, the dauphin.

A few years later, in the fall of 1984, two other chelas traveled to Paris on another mission from the masters. Ruth Hawkins went there with another devotee, anchoring the light at the request of her twin flame, Paul the Venetian. They rented an apartment where they decreed for France every day for four months, morning, afternoon and evening. You can read the story of her experiences in *The Masters and Their Retreats*.

Ruth's example is something any one of us can emulate. She always carried with her a stack of the wallet-sized Chart of Your Divine Self. Whenever she got the chance, she would give a Chart to someone. By the time she left Paris, many of the artists had a picture of the Chart on their easels. Ruth and her friend also did many violet-flame decrees—half an hour three times a day. They felt that there was much hardness in the city and that the violet flame was needed to soften it so that the people would accept the light. Every Thursday the two women held a vigil for the youth.[20]

Ruth is now an ascended lady master. Her twin flame is the chohan of the third ray of divine love. He is hierarch of the Château de Liberté, his retreat on the etheric plane over southern France on the Rhône River. Paul sponsors the ascended master culture for this age and works with all who desire to bring that culture forth on behalf of mankind.

Even today to establish a center for the ascended masters

in a city is an important goal. There is no greater service that you can render your city and nation than to establish a center, however humble, to keep the flame at the altar and to receive the new students on behalf of the ascended masters. It is no small undertaking, but it has great rewards.

Jophiel and Christine spoke of this in their dictation:

> Blessed hearts, there has been a great staying action by the focus of light in New Delhi.* Vortices of energy penetrating Asia have made all the difference in the balance of power East and West. With the raising up of teaching centers in the cities of the earth, there is hope to the entire Great White Brotherhood for miracles upon miracles to occur upon earth.
>
> I pray then that you will not count the personal cost in your life—not the cost of sacrifice or service or surrender or that selflessness which is the requirement of the hour.[21]

In a few cities of the world, the ascended masters themselves maintain physical focuses for their service. One such retreat is in the city of Paris, where a master known simply as the Master of Paris maintains a retreat (its true function unknown to the outer world), which he often visits in a physical form. The messengers have said that this retreat

> ... is a beautiful old castle-like residence with many windows overlooking the city of Paris. This focus is kept up by his disciples and is used frequently by the masters as a meeting place in Paris from which they can direct the energies necessary to hold the balance for the governments of Europe.

* The Ashram of the World Mother was established on April 17, 1980.

El Morya has spoken of the desire of Saint Germain to have physical focuses of light in the cities of the world, like that of the Master of Paris: "Saint Germain is not content to train the souls in the etheric retreats of the Great White Brotherhood. No, he is determined to have the focuses such as the focus of the Master of Paris, a home of light in the physical octave, a home of light in the city, a home of light where souls can be received."[22] The masters need students to maintain these focuses. Morya asked for the stalwart ones, the builders and the pioneers to come forth.[23]

Accepting Help from Others

Annice commented one day about a person who would not accept help from another, even if she was sick or in need of help. She said:

We need to accept help from others. I learned this when recovering from my heart surgery and I had to put on these tight anti-embolic stockings every day. I simply could not pull them up myself. So every day I called Susan Kulp and she would come over and pull my stockings onto my legs.

Annice laughed as she recalled the situation. It had been humbling and she was a private person, but she was also grateful for the help that Susan had provided for her.

Often the masters will contrive situations where we are forced to accept help from others. The first Mother of the Flame, Clara Louise, suffered an illness at the conclusion of her life so she could learn that she needed to graciously accept the help of others.

Ascended Lady Master Clara Louise was embodied as Clara Louise Kieninger in her last life—a student of the ascended masters and the first Mother of the Flame of the

Keepers of the Flame Fraternity. Clara Louise had been the apostle James at the time of Jesus. She wrote her life story in the book *Ich Dien,* which provides an insight into one soul's journey on the spiritual path prior to the ascension.

Training Your Replacement

Mother said to me, "I want you to train everyone in that department how you do what you do. Who is the next person in line to take over Office of Ministry?"

I named a person who I was working with at the time and who was helpful to me in administration and other types of work.

Mother continued, "Every time you are on the phone, have her there. Every time you counsel or solve a problem, I want her to know exactly what you do. She is to become your shadow."

This statement reminded me of my own experience with Mark. I recall when I used to sit in Mark's office. I was his correspondence secretary, but I never wrote a letter. Mark would look at all of his correspondence and I would file it. I filled a four-drawer cabinet full of what I considered to be junk—such things as catalogs on belts, wallets and shirts.

When I questioned him about this, Mark said, "You don't know when I might need it." He would not allow me to throw any of it away, even though I protested that some of it was three years old and he could not possibly need it.

After he passed I realized that all of the filing that I did had another purpose. He was simply keeping me in his presence, keeping me close to him. As he disciplined people or taught them or answered people's questions, I was listening and being trained, even though outwardly I was just in the room filing.

Never Above the Law

At Mother's direction, Annice one year gave a lecture at Summit University about Mother's embodiments. Mother was listening in the sacristy as Annice was describing the life in France where she was embodied as a washerwoman who lived a very ordinary life. Mark Prophet was embodied as a wandering priest who administered extreme unction right before she passed from the screen of life.

As he administered last rites, Mother looked into his eyes, recognized him as her twin flame, and realized that she could have done much more with that life. Her dying words were, *"Une autre opportunité!"*—another opportunity, another chance to embody and fulfill her mission.

Mother had said that this was a life of little consequence, where she accomplished very little—essentially a wasted life. Annice described what happened when she gave this explanation to the students:

I said that this was not one of Mother's major lifetimes. She had been a washerwoman who spent most of her life doing her laundry and speaking with her neighbors over the back fence, never going farther than about eight blocks from her home.

After a little while Mother came out on the platform, sent

222

everyone on a break, and asked to see me and the Teaching Assistants in the sacristy. She said to me, "I'll have you know that it was a very important life. It was a major life. I raised eight children in that life. Now you go back and tell them that it was an important life. I raised eight children!"

I was never above the law. All of my disciplines were public. Perhaps Mother said it for those in the audience who were bringing up children. She understood the importance of bringing children into the world.

Mother herself described this as a wasted life, but she scolded Annice for saying the same thing, and I have wondered why.

Perhaps it was the emphasis that Annice placed on the story. When Mother described this life, her sense that it was wasted seemed to be that she could have done so much more than "talking over the back fence." I don't know how Annice told the story, but she might have somehow implied that raising eight children was a waste of time. This was not what Mother meant, and it might have been a very wrong message for some of the students in particular.

In a larger sense, Mother's teaching to a particular audience was always specific to those people, but also universal in scope and application. The truths were timeless, but she might present them in different ways with different emphases to different groups of people at different times. On one occasion a student at Summit University asked for an explanation of the fall of man. Mother explained that she had been asked this many times, and each time the master had given a different explanation, one that was specific to the person who asked the question. A critic might see these different explanations as contradictory. Someone with a higher vision might see them as different facets of a larger truth.

It is important to remember that we can't be rote in sharing the teachings with others. We need the sensitivity to the Holy Spirit, not only to deliver an accurate teaching, but also to deliver the specific teaching that is needed by a particular person or audience. Mother speaks of this as the gift of the Holy Spirit of speaking in tongues. When we have this gift, those who hear us speak will hear the teaching in a language they can understand and assimilate.

Giving Up Chocolate

One time in Minneapolis, Morya gave a direction to the staff that he did not want them to be eating chocolate. It was a private message just to the staff. I was not present, but when they came home, they told me, "We can't eat chocolate." I said, "Nonsense. Till I hear it myself, I will keep eating it."

Well, the next day the message was played, and I was obedient. It was hard because I loved to drink hot chocolate. I did not like coffee but I sure liked hot chocolate. Since that day, however, I have never knowingly eaten chocolate. I have a certain amount of obedience either built in to me or bashed into me.

In 2001, I saw a documentary about Catholic monasteries in Brazil and how, centuries ago, they developed a liking for cocoa. The monks would mix the cocoa with herbs and drink it. The nuns did not like the taste until one enterprising nun mixed it with vanilla, and then they loved it. They drank it a lot, became virtually intoxicated, and did not do any work. It became almost like a drug to them. The local abbot wrote to Rome and said that the nuns were incorrigible. This prompted an edict from the Vatican that there would be no more cocoa drinking in the monasteries and nunneries in Brazil.

When I saw the documentary I was quite sure that I was involved in some way. I could imagine that Morya had been somewhere in the hierarchy of the church and I had been a disobedient nun. And here, centuries later, was Morya telling me again for a second time, not to eat chocolate.

In researching this book I found out that Cardinal Mazarin was responsible for first popularizing chocolate in France. So it is possible that Annice had more than one karmic connection with chocolate in her past.

Why did Morya ask the staff not to eat chocolate? We don't have his complete explanation. However, chocolate is known to affect brain function, having mood-elevating effects. In recent years it has also been found that chocolate contains relatively high concentrations of lead, having the potential to cause mild lead poisoning, especially in children.

Morya told Mother that when you take chocolate into your system, depending on the level of purity in your body and the amount of spiritual work that you do, it can take from seven to fourteen days for you to rid yourself of the impact of this substance in your body. If you eat a heavier diet and do less spiritual work, it may take a longer time.

For Annice, however, what was of most importance was the master's word. It was a sacrifice for her to give up something that she enjoyed, but it was a small sacrifice compared with the blessings she received on the path.

Working in the Candy Store

On the way back from a late breakfast I posted a package for Annice, a coat that she had ordered by mail order. Unfortunately the coat did not fit, so she was returning it. But even the least expensive way cost $7.15. She bemoaned the cost and said:

I remember when postcards cost a penny. At that time I worked at Woolworths for 33 cents an hour. I did forty-eight hours a week, amounting to the huge sum of $16, and this bought a lot in those days. This was in the time when a meal cost very little, a movie ticket was a quarter, and for $15 per month you could pay your home mortgage or rent a nice two-bedroom home.

I worked in stationary. One day the girl in the candy section next door was ill, so the manager asked me to move over to that section, which I did. I liked it a lot. He asked me one day what I thought of the candy that was the special for that week. I said, "When I have the funds to buy some, I'll taste it."

He said, "You mean you haven't tried it?"

I said, "Well, no."

"Now listen here, young lady. I expect you to try the candy so that you can encourage the customers to buy it."

Not quite believing, I said, "You mean I should eat the candy?"

"Of course. I expect you to. You are required to eat the candy so that you can recommend it."

Well, I liked that a lot, and in the three months before my wedding, I went from 104 to 116 pounds.

Annice grew up in the Depression, and like many people of that era, she really appreciates the value of a dollar. She has always been very careful to use money wisely, whether her own personal funds or those of the organization.

She has taught courses on abundance and written a book called *Secrets of Prosperity*. She knows that one of the principles of abundance is that God will give us more abundance if we use wisely what we already have.

There is a big difference between being frugal and having the "poverty consciousness." Annice has the consciousness of the abundance of God and trusts God to take care of her needs, and she is a good steward of God's resources. She is also generous and not afraid to spend money for a good purpose, but she is not extravagant or wasteful.

An example of this is her clothes. She once commented that her clothes and belongings never seemed to wear out, but she never held on to things for too long. She might keep some particularly nice item for a few years longer, but mostly she rotated her wardrobe and donated old clothes to the senior citizens center in Livingston.

Annice understands that there is a spiritual science having to do with clothes and how they affect our aura. We represent the ascended masters to the world and our clothing can carry spiritual light. Even the matter and the molecules of old clothing can become tired and no longer a vessel to hold that light. Old clothes carry an old vibration and the records of our consciousness when we wore them years earlier. We may have changed our vibration over the years, but if we keep the same old clothes, we may be limiting the expression of our new self.

Morya says in the "Heart, Head and Hand Decrees," "I AM changing all my garments, old ones for the bright new day ..." We need to do this physically as well as spiritually, and renew our wardrobe from time to time.

Annice tried to encourage a friend to also change her wardrobe, but this friend insisted on wearing the same dresses year after year because they were "still good." She kept her old nightdresses until they were threadbare and almost frayed, not because she could not afford to buy something new but due to a latent lack of self worth. Long lifetimes of vows of poverty in nunneries had taken their toll on this friend's sense of self, and Annice could never convince her to change her ways.

All My Gals Ascended

One day in day in late 2002, Annice was reminiscing about all of the ladies that she had worked with on staff at Santa Barbara. Her friend and former staff member Anita Buchanan had just passed, and Annice was feeling the loss. Annice had worked with Helen MacDonald, Patricia Johnson, Ruth Hawkins, Helen Ries and Marguerite Baker, all of whom had made their ascension. Edith Emmert had passed in 1988, and in 1990 Lanello said she was working hard at inner levels to qualify as a candidate for the ascension.

Evelyn Dykman had also passed recently, and Annice felt sure that she had or would ascend—although we did not find out for sure because the messenger was no longer confirming these things on the outer. And now Anita was gone, after a long illness and time spent in a nursing home. Annice felt that Anita would ascend. Even if she had some remaining karma, she would be able to balance it from inner levels.

In her last weeks, Anita had said, "Saint Germain, get me out of here!" And he had. It must have been a difficult existence for her, and at last she was free from the bondage of earth and her body. Anita had been embodied as Queen Isabella, the Spanish monarch who supported Christopher Columbus (an embodiment of the master Saint Germain).

I had not known these women, although I had met Helen

Ries and Patricia Johnson. I wanted to know more about them. Annice told me about them over lunch:

All of my gals from Santa Barbara have ascended, except me. And I just have to keep writing books and books and books.

Mark had told me to look after or look out for some of them and so I did. I visited Anita in the convalescent home whenever I could, which was not often. I kept an eye out for her.

It is funny how I miss her. Even though I saw her very little in recent years and she could remember very little when I spoke to her, I miss her presence. We must have known each other way back. It is an old tie. Anita was the last one of the Santa Barbara group to pass on.

Mark also asked me to look out for Helen MacDonald. Helen had been on staff at Santa Barbara. She was a retired PhD in zoology and was very health-minded. She had started the first co-op in Berkeley, California, years ago. She had used her entire fortune traveling and giving lectures about the health dangers of fluoride in water supplies, and Mark said that she almost single-handedly kept the major cities of the United States free of fluoride in the water. They only fluoridated the water after Helen left embodiment.

Helen lived with me and Lester for several years in the Motherhouse in Santa Barbara. We moved out when our rooms were needed for more office space. The three of us moved to a house on a steep hill.

One day, Helen was coming home carrying a tray of food for her dinner. She got out of her car and forgot to set the handbrake. She tried to grab the handbrake as the car began to roll down the hill, and somehow she was drawn under the car and it rolled over her leg. There was a huge blood blister. Lester and I got her in the house and called the doctor.

We took her to a private hospital in Los Angeles. The doctors were saying that her leg would need to be amputated —but Helen would have none of it. She treated it with vitamin E ointment and it completely healed. She later went with me to live at the San Francisco Teaching Center. During that time she continued her work with the Cancer Society of Los Angeles, where her daughter was president.

At one time we all thought that Helen was having a heart attack, and she was taken to a hospital in San Francisco. She was told that she had a serious heart condition. Eventually Helen went to live with her daughter. I then felt that she was out of my hands. Later Helen went to Georgia for chelation therapy, but sadly, she died during the therapy, which was brand new in those days.

I called to talk about the funeral arrangements, knowing that Helen had not wanted to be embalmed or buried and that she would not have wanted an autopsy unless it was essential or the cause of her death was in question. All of this was stated in her will. When I spoke to the funeral director, he spoke in his southern accent and said, "She looks beautiful."

Alarmed, I said in a low voice, "What do you mean?"

I was horrified to learn that Helen had been embalmed.

I proclaimed, "But Helen's will stated she was *not* to be embalmed!"

Unperturbed, the funeral director went on to say, "She looks beautiful. We had to have her look beautiful. And by the way, the autopsy did not show any sign of cancer."

I was appalled. I took charge and said, "Well, she must be

cremated!"

The funeral director emphatically said, with his broad Southern accent, "Ma'am, we don't *burn* our people *here*."

And I, just as emphatic, said, "Well, you are going to burn this one!" They fussed and fumed for three or four days, but finally Helen was cremated.

I take the masters' instruction very seriously and in the midst of all this I was quite distraught. I went to Mother and said, "I've probably blown her ascension and mine too because she has been embalmed."

Mother calmed me and said, "I'll talk to Saint Germain about it."

And that was when we received the teaching, "The flame of the Holy Spirit can change time and space and she can still ascend."

I was overjoyed to hear this teaching, because I thought that I had wrecked it for my friend. Even though I had no control over the events in Helen's life, I still had a sense of responsibility and I took Mark's charge to me seriously.

Mother asked me to conduct Helen's memorial service, which I did. There was a wonderful and joyous service filled with songs to the ascension and decrees. Mother had seen Helen after her passing, looking radiant, and had told everyone that she had ascended. What a joy! Another of the masters' and messengers' students graduated.

The next day Mother came to me and said, "Helen has not ascended. I saw her in her light body and I thought she was ascended, but she is not yet ascended. I am sure that she will in time, but she isn't yet. We will just have to keep it as a secret between us."

So we did. Five years later, when George Lancaster

ascended, Mother confirmed that Helen was ascended too. Whether that meant that Helen had waited five years at inner levels completing the requirements for the ascension, I don't know. But finally it was confirmed that all was well and Helen was ascended.

Helen's sister Persis had ascended years earlier.

Helen was the one who got me into the habit of afternoon naps. I wondered if this was a secret of her longevity. She loved to work and always needed something to do for service to the masters. As long as she had that, she felt that she could go on forever. And we all hoped that she would.

In *The Masters and the Spiritual Path* the messengers have explained the benefits to the ongoing soul when the physical form is cremated following transition:

> The problem of disposing of the physical body arises at the time of transition, or death. Not all are able to ascend physically as did Elijah, for the actual raising of the physical body into the atmosphere occurs only when the individual has achieved a certain degree of self-mastery before the transition is made....
>
> Those who do not raise their physical bodies at the time of their passing may ascend from inner levels, elevating the etheric, mental and emotional bodies together with their soul consciousness. This may occur immediately or within twenty-four to seventy-two hours thereafter, or even from several months to several decades as the Law may require.
>
> Whether the soul ascends leaving behind the physical body or prepares at inner levels for reembodiment, the physical body must pass through the natural

process of dissolution. Therefore, in order to facilitate the soul's transition to higher octaves, either to complete the requirements for the ascension or to enter into temple training for the next life, Serapis Bey has recommended that the physical body be placed on ice for a period of three days after death and that it then be cremated....

Through this ancient ritual, the light in the heart of the physical atoms is released by the fire element, and the energy that was used to sustain the form is immediately returned to the heart of the God Presence.... Cremation eliminates the possibility of the form exercising dominion over the soul through what is called residual magnetism; for the records of the individual's thoughts and feelings do leave a residue of substance that creates a magnetic forcefield in the body even after interment, which tends to keep the soul earthbound....

[If cremation is impossible for legal or other reasons,] it should be remembered that the power of the Holy Spirit, when invoked through the violet flame, is able to transmute body, mind and soul, including the cause, effect, record and memory of all that is left of the human, wherever it may appear in the earth's crust. Truly the universal grace of God is sufficient for man's salvation.[24]

CHAPTER 4

Annice as I Have Known Her

Sometimes people ask me, "What is Annice really like?"

Those who know her would surely say that Annice is one of a kind—unique in many ways. She has been a student and disciple of the ascended masters for many decades. She has a vast storehouse of experience and knowledge of their teachings to draw upon. But all of this is presented in a seemingly ordinary outer package—with all of its human idiosyncrasies. Annice never did fit the traditional image of a saint or a holy person, and she did not try to.

When we are in human form, all of us—the saints included—are subject to the ups and downs of the human condition. This was true of the Guru, and it was true of Annice. Like any of us, Annice could go through days when she seemed covered over by the outcropping of the impurities from within. Then the sun would shine, the light of the Presence or of a master might be with her, the sacred fire would consume the darkness of the human condition, and she might appear to be more of a saint than she really was. So we cannot go by the outer condition in either case, because it is the totality of one's being—

the seen and what is unseen to outer eyes—that is weighed in the day of judgment.

So to answer the question that opened this chapter, all I can do is return to my experience of working with her over many years.

Some people loved her. Most admired and respected her. There were also a few who hated her.

When working with her she could be very direct at times—"white ray," as she would say. She rarely minced words. If she had nothing to say, she said nothing. If she had something to say, she often just said it—direct, straightforward, without amplification. It was not unusual to hear her say, "Dear heart, that's your ego talking." Or to a student trying to slip quietly into the Summit University classroom after one of her lectures had begun, "Young man, you are late."

Sometimes, by worldly standards, or even by the standards of other chelas, her methods could be viewed as severe. On the other hand, she could also be a model of tact and diplomacy when this was necessary.

Did she have faults? She certainly did. Like all of us she had her shortcomings. She could be stubborn and unbending, and she knew it. Often it was a good kind of stubborn, born of an inner knowing. If she said, "I know with all the knowing in me," then you knew she was not going to be moved on that subject.

Some coworkers found her difficult to get on with. The most important thing to understand was that it was her show. If you could do things her way, everything would usually be fine.

Her discernment and attunement could be astute. Sometimes she would read the vibration and sum up a situation very quickly and be quite sure that she was right. She was never one to compromise principles, and she could be like a dog with a bone if something was of concern to her.

In spite of her good attunement, however, she was not always right—but she was never one to dwell on mistakes, her own or other people's. If she found she was wrong about something, she admitted it freely, and sometimes with amusement. She could let go of things and situations with surprising speed.

She was not afraid to act. She was not afraid to make a decision. She was a tactician and a strategist. She almost always had a plan and she worked her plan.

There was no one better in a crisis than Annice. She was a calming presence with great faith in God. You could bring her a calamity, and although her concern was genuine, she seemed to take a larger view. She might give a few comments, say, "What a pity, dear," and ask a few pertinent questions. A lesson learned, an example given, a teaching shared. But the burden of the problem was never dwelt upon. Scarcely missing a beat, she simply carried on with the work—and expected that you would too.

Annice has a long memory. She does not forget a kindness or gift. Similarly, if the masters or the messengers gave an instruction, if the inner direction was clear or the prompting of the master was present, or if it was simply the right thing to do in her eyes, she did it. She didn't need to be told twice.

Her deep faith was always evident. When someone brought a problem to her, she often suggested, "Ask Morya." The masters were a very real presence in her life. Even though she didn't see them (or if she did, she never let on), she made the masters, and later their messengers, come alive for others. She prayed and decreed. She gave an hour of violet flame faithfully every day in the later years of her life, until her stroke prevented it.

Annice had a medical condition called spinal stenosis, which meant that she developed tiredness and pain in her back and legs if she stood for too long. So she was most often seated and did not stand or walk more than was necessary. This had an interesting effect: when people came to visit or work with her, it was almost as if she was receiving an audience at court.

Ministers, attorneys, doctors, simple folk, mothers and fathers came to her for advice, and she dispensed it without ceremony. She looked you directly in the eye, straightened her clothes and then gave a direct response.

Annice has always been very capable. She can get things done. But through all of this there remains a child-like quality to her spirit. She delights in small things. If you want to see her face light up, just say the magic words "strawberry short-cake." She loves a good turkey dinner. She loves the changing seasons. She loves Christmas. She loves flowers and birds. She has seen and done much, and yet she enjoys the snow and the sunshine, the green grass and the scenery along the highway. When she is out in nature, her voice takes on a quality of delight in the creator and the creation.

She was a lady who loved to go out for lunch. (She still does, but she is not quite as mobile as she used to be.) An outing with Annice was always a little ritual. Don't forget her walking stick, and you must have the blanket to cover her knees in the car. You carry her purse, pillow or anything else she might need for the journey. You open the door and wait by the side of the car while she gets in, you put her handbag at her feet, cover her knees with the blanket and help with her seatbelt. Then off to the adventure of the day.

As you sallied forth to Yellowstone Park or for a luncheon engagement, it was almost as if the problems of the world, or at least your little part of it, were on hold and you could enter another era. On those outings it was easy to see her as a queen in a past life. She commanded respect. "Young man. We have been here twenty minutes and have not yet been waited upon."

For many years she lived in what some would consider to be humble circumstances—very happy in her two small rooms with a little patch of garden outside, surrounded by a white picket fence. She was quite content with simple pleasures. There was a wind chime beside her door. Rabbits and squirrels and deer came to visit.

One of Annice's joys was her garden. She loved to plant flowers and watch them grow. She would notice every little flower, even the tiny purple-and-yellow Johnny-jump-ups that grew beside the door or in the grate. She got frustrated when deer would jump her fence and eat her precious flowers.

She took weekend drives to Yellowstone Park with her friend Marilyn Barrick, until Marilyn passed on. Annice loved the wildlife, especially the buffalo. Seeing a bison by the road, she would say, "Isn't he beautiful? He's my friend."

After her stroke she moved to a quiet home in North Glastonbury overlooking her beloved mountains. When she was not working on a book, she would spend hours watching the birds that came to feed on the deck.

All her life, Annice has been practical and not wasteful with funds. She had few possessions, by worldly standards, and yet she appreciated the good things of life. She had excellent taste in furnishings and decorations. She seemed to want for nothing. She had that rare gift of contentment with her life.

How different to her life as Mary, Queen of Scots, or Cardinal Mazarin. Her current life was one of service, and she liked it that way. She had a quiet happiness about her—rarely in a bad mood, fairly balanced, and mostly with a peaceful perspective based on a long life. She could sometimes be uplifting to be around, almost like a tonic. She took you back to a time when life was good and choices were clear.

Probably more than anything, Annice loves the masters and the messengers. She has dedicated her life to their mission. Every day she has to do something that furthers the mission, else to her way of thinking there is no point to being in embodiment. Although she has not seen Mother in recent years, she is still a chela of the Guru. Out of sight is never out of mind. Their love has endured and never diminished.

In some ways, Annice found the culmination of her own mission in her seventies and eighties as she worked with Summit University Press, publishing the teachings of the masters. Up until the time of her stroke, she wrote in her neat fluid handwriting in pencil or pen on a yellow pad of paper. And she signed her name LD, for Lady Dorcas, the name that Saint Germain had given her through Mark.

She took the responsibility of working on publications very seriously, but also with the simplicity and humility that was her nature. She would occasionally say, "Who am I to do this? I did not finish a college education." When she sat down to work on a book, she asked the master to show her what she needed to know. I recall her sitting down to do her final edits on *Walking with the Master,* asking Jesus to show her if there was anything that was not to his liking, any problem or inconsistency. By seeking this attunement with the masters, she could often go right to a problem.

Perhaps her greatest achievement of those later years was the completion of the Climb the Highest Mountain series. Annice spent the early years of her training and service on staff working on this project, and the first volume, containing the first seven chapters, was published in 1972. Her concluding years on staff seemed to complete the cycle, with the final volume, chapters 29 to 33, being published in 2008.

For those of us who have seen her dedication to the path over the years, there never seemed to be a doubt that Annice would make it in the end. You could feel it in her aura. And yet she was always humble and never took this for granted. She knew that the ascension is a gift and it is offered by grace.

If Annice has one defining quality, it might be endurance—a strength of character and dedication to the spiritual path that is seldom seen. It is a quality that has served her well.

In some ways she has been like a rock, never moving with the storms of life. It is as if she has always been there—faithful, consistent, constant and stalwart. Troubles might come and go, people arrive and depart, but under all kinds of circumstances you got the feeling that deep down she was never really moved much by the things of this world. Perhaps this is one reason she was so trusted by the messengers.

Reverend Annice Booth,
Lady Dorcas,
Co-worker of the Darjeeling Council,
Student of El Morya and Serapis Bey,
Chela of the messengers Mark and Mother,

Your friends and co-workers from the Summit Lighthouse and Church Universal and Triumphant around the world salute you!

From the Guru to the Chela

On the following pages are four personal messages from Mother to Annice. These cards give another glimpse into the relationship between Guru and chela.

———————————

The first is from a card written around 1979, following a difficult period in Mother's life.

To my beloved Mother and Friend

Dearest Annice,
    What have I done to deserve you, my dearest friend—especially in the past two years. May the angels keep you here till all who are to ascend have fulfilled their reason for being.
    God bless you for ever.

                            Dearest Friend

The second message is from a birthday card to Annice five years after her heart attack. This was Annice's seventy-third birthday. It accompanied the gift of a heart-shaped floral wreath.

On the envelope:

To dear Annice
  Blossoms of your Heart will bear fruit to a world!
                                    Elizabeth

In the card:

                    May 28, 1993

Beloved Annice,
  God has given back to you your blessed heart. With every day may the zeal of the Lord multiply your service. Please receive this heart as a focus of your eternal heart and life and know that every leaf and petal bears the love and greetings of a special angelic Messenger.
  With birthday greetings from our dear Mark and the ascended hierarchy I add my own. You are a blessed Mother to me and to all our Teaching Centers and Study Groups.
  Just how precious you are is beyond words.
  All my love and gratitude forever,

                                    —Mother

The third message is from a card to Annice on her seventy-fifth birthday

May 28, 1995

Beloved Annice,
Heaven records your magnanimous service over years and lifetimes. We are grateful.

All my love,
Mother

The fourth message is written inside a copy of the book *Jesus, CEO*, by Laurie Beth Jones, the gift that accompanied this card.

May 28, 1995

Beloved Annice,
May God bless and prosper your cause: the delivery of truth to mankind.
All our love and gratitude and support,

Mother
& El Morya

33 Keys for the Practical Mystic

Little keys unlock the biggest doors, and man must be ready to walk through and not stand hesitatingly upon the threshold.

—EL MORYA

Thirty-three keys from conversations with Mrs. Booth:

1. You need a teacher.
2. Change is essential. If you were already perfect, you wouldn't still be here.
3. Watch out for false teachers. Beware of flattery.
4. What you eat is important. You need your body to be able to balance your karma.
5. When the Guru asks you to do something, don't say no.
6. Spiritual experiences may happen. Don't be attached.
7. Don't try to do it all yourself. Allow God to work through you.
8. Trust your own attunement, but always be willing to listen to others.

9. You have lived before. Don't be attached.

10. When you run into a problem, make the call.

11. Know when a project is finished.

12. Accept correction well.

13. You did some good things in past lives. You did some bad things too. Don't be attached to either.

14. Be where you need to be. Mobility is the sign of the chela.

15. No matter what happens, keep your harmony.

16. Trust no man. Trust only God.

17. Don't let your ego get in the way.

18. "I can't" means "I won't."

19. Let go of family mesmerism.

20. Don't personalize your work.

21. Study the masters' teachings.

22. Observe what is happening around you.

23. Stay in your body. There is work to do.

24. Don't condemn others.

25. There are things you won't have time for if you are serious about the path.

26. "If the messenger be an ant, heed him!"

27. Be smart about your spiritual work.

28. Recharge when you need to.

29. Be willing to accept help from others.

30. Train your replacement.

31. Be willing to surrender your indulgences.

32. Look out for others.

33. Be humble before God, positive to the world.

FURTHER READING

On the Guru-chela relationship:

Paramahansa Yogananda, *Autobiography of a Yogi.* Self-Realization Fellowship

Will Garver, *Brother of the Third Degree.* Borden

Elizabeth Clare Prophet, *Community.* Summit University Press

Charles Leadbeater, *The Masters and the Path.* Theosophical Publishing House

Elizabeth Clare Prophet, *Walking with the Master.* Summit University Press

On the ascended masters:

Mark L. Prophet and Elizabeth Clare Prophet, *The Masters and Their Retreats.* Summit University Press

Mark L. Prophet and Elizabeth Clare Prophet, Climb the Highest Mountain series (nine volumes). Summit University Press

Godfre Ray King, *Unveiled Mysteries.* Saint Germain Press

NOTES

1. Saint Germain, December 12, 1984, "The Harvest," *Pearls of Wisdom (PoW)*, vol. 27, no. 61.
2. Djwal Kul, October 12, 1998, *PoW*, vol. 41, no. 50.
3. Lanello, March 1, 1992, "How to Ascend," *PoW*, vol. 35, no. 10.
4. The Great Divine Director, November 5, 1966, *PoW 1969*, pp. 263–65.
5. Seraphic Meditations I, II and III were later published in the book *Dossier on the Ascension*, by Serapis Bey. The words have also been put to music as song 302A in *The Summit Lighthouse Book of Songs*.
6. Amitabha, January 2, 1994, "Mantra is Empowerment," *PoW*, vol. 37, no. 8.
7. Mark L. Prophet and Elizabeth Clare Prophet, *The Path of the Higher Self* (Gardiner, Mont.: Summit University Press, 2003), p. 443.
8. Marguerite Baker, *And Then the Angels Came to the First Grade Children* (Gardiner, Mont.: The Summit Lighthouse, 1975).
9. Lanello, "How to Ascend."
10. Ibid.
11. Matt. 25:40.
12. El Morya, February 3, 1985, "Chela—Christed One—Guru," *PoW*, vol. 28, no. 11.
13. Rev. 11:3.
14. Matt. 12:50.
15. Matt. 10:36.
16. Kuthumi, January 27, 1985, "Remember the Ancient Encounter," *PoW*, vol. 28, no. 9.
17. El Morya, *The Chela and the Path* (Gardiner, Mont.: Summit University Press, 1976), p. 70.
18. Lanello, "How to Ascend."
19. Jophiel and Christine, January 1, 1981, "For Europe: A Dispensation and a Cycle," *PoW*, vol. 24, no. 12.
20. Mark L. Prophet and Elizabeth Clare Prophet, *The Masters and Their Retreats*, s.v. "Ruth Hawkins."
21. Jophiel and Christine, "For Europe: A Dispensation and a Cycle."
22. El Morya, November 23, 1975, "The Precipitation of the Diamond of the Will of God," in Elizabeth Clare Prophet, *The Greater Way of Freedom* (Gardiner, Mont.: Summit University Press, 2009), p. 76.
23. *The Masters and Their Retreats*, s.v. "The Master of Paris."
24. Mark L. Prophet and Elizabeth Clare Prophet, *The Masters and the Spiritual Path* (Gardiner, Mont.: Summit University Press, 2001), pp. 123, 124, 126. Additional teaching on cremation may be found in *The Path to Immortality* (Gardiner, Mont.: Summit University Press, 2006), pp. 318–25.

Printed in the United States
220379BV00001B/4/P

9 780982 499702